Bridge Club Player's Quiz Book

Raymond & Sally Brock

B. T. Batsford, *London*

First published 2002

© Raymond & Sally Brock 2002

ISBN 0 7134 8716 X

A CIP catalogue record for this book is available from the British Library.

Typeset by Wakewing, High Wycombe
Printed by Creative Print & Design, Ebbw Vale, Wales
for the publishers,
B. T. Batsford, 64 Brewery Road,
London N7 9NT
A member of the Chrysalis Group plc

Batsford books by the same authors:

By Raymond Brock
Step by Step: Planning the Defence
Expert Defence
How to Play Bridge: No-Trump Play

By Sally Brock
Step by Step: Overcalls
Step by Step: Suit Combinations
How to Play Bridge: Playing with Trumps
Bridge for Absolute Beginners *(with Robert Sheehan)*

By Raymond & Sally Brock
Expert Tuition for Tournament Bridge
Bridge Quiz: Slam Play
Bridge Quiz: Bidding
Bridge Quiz: Defence

A BATSFORD BRIDGE BOOK
Series Editor: Phil King

INTRODUCTION

The problems in this book are taken from real life, either from hands we ourselves have played, or from tournament or international play – not that international players get every hand right by a long chalk. The hands are not contrived to make a point but are occasionally modified to make the point clearer. There is not always a clear-cut solution; sometimes you have to choose between reasonable, alternative lines.

As in real life, some freaks do occur but not too many. Again, as in real life, you meet a variety of opponents: those who overbid maniacally and those timid players who persistently underbid; and those who misplay the hand, allowing you to demonstrate your unsleeping defensive accuracy.

Also you meet various bidding methods whilst you yourself stick to your weak no-trump four-card major base – although your system is incidental to the problems themselves. You do, however, adopt the modern practice when holding the ace-king of a suit of leading the ace for attitude and the king for count. From length you lead fourth highest, or second highest from poor suits.

The problems are graded so that those in Part One (problems 1 to 20) are simple, whilst those in Part Two (problems 21 to 40) are more challenging. The problems in Part Three (41 to 60) are quite difficult – in some cases extremely difficult.

There is a concentration on problems involving defence and play, but there are other aspects to bridge. You will therefore find some problems concerned with the lead and others to do with selection of the best call.

PART ONE

Problem 1

Game All. Dealer North.

♠ 842
♡ A1074
◇ AKQJ10
♣ Q

♠ 9763
♡ QJ5
◇ 53
♣ AK43

West	North	East	South
–	1◇	Pass	1♠
Pass	2♡	Pass	3NT
All Pass			

Against your three no-trumps, West leads the king of spades. East overtakes with the ace and returns a spade. West takes three more tricks in the suit before switching to a low club. Over to you.

Solution 1

Game All. Dealer North.

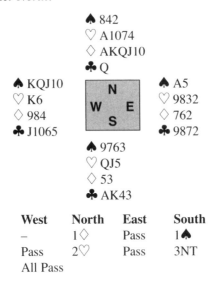

♠ 842
♡ A1074
◇ AKQJ10
♣ Q

♠ KQJ10
♡ K6
◇ 984
♣ J1065

♠ A5
♡ 9832
◇ 762
♣ 9872

♠ 9763
♡ QJ5
◇ 53
♣ AK43

West	North	East	South
–	1◇	Pass	1♠
Pass	2♡	Pass	3NT
All Pass			

Against your three no-trumps, West leads the king of spades. East overtakes with the ace and returns a spade. West takes three more tricks in the suit before switching to a low club. Over to you.

A quick trick count reveals that you have nine tricks: five diamonds, three clubs and the ace of hearts. Can you see any problems?

The problem is that the club suit is blocked. If you win the queen in dummy, there is no way to reach your hand to cash your ace and king.

You have to hope that West has the king of hearts. Overtake dummy's queen of clubs with your king and run the queen of hearts. If it holds you are home, with two clubs and two hearts (or one club and three hearts) to go with dummy's five diamonds; if it loses you will go down, but at least you gave yourself a chance.

One of the most important considerations on any hand is: 'Do I have the entries?' If you remember to ask yourself the question you are better placed to find the answer.

Problem 2

Love All. Pairs. Dealer South.

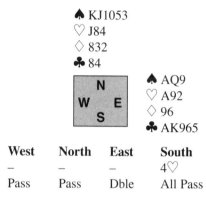

♠ KJ1053
♡ J84
◇ 832
♣ 84

♠ AQ9
♡ A92
◇ 96
♣ AK965

West	North	East	South
–	–	–	4♡
Pass	Pass	Dble	All Pass

Your double of South's four heart opening was for penalty, so it was not surprising that your partner passed it. Dummy is weak, so you probably have the values for game and it may not be sufficient simply to beat the doubled game.

Plan the defence on the queen of clubs lead.

Solution 2

Love All. Pairs. Dealer South.

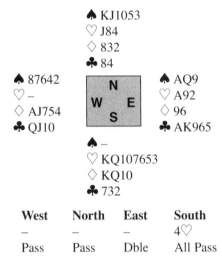

♠ KJ1053
♡ J84
◇ 832
♣ 84

♠ 87642
♡ –
◇ AJ754
♣ QJ10

♠ AQ9
♡ A92
◇ 96
♣ AK965

♠ –
♡ KQ107653
◇ KQ10
♣ 732

West	North	East	South
–	–	–	4♡
Pass	Pass	Dble	All Pass

Your double of four hearts was for penalty, so it was not surprising that your partner passed it. Dummy is weak, so you probably have the values for game and it may not be sufficient simply to beat the doubled game.

Plan the defence on the queen of clubs lead.

It may look tempting to win the king of clubs and switch to your doubleton diamond. This will be successful if partner has the ace-queen, generating an immediate ruff. However, if he has A10xxx, partner will need to duck his ace to give us a later ruff – not a certainty. Alternatively, it could be right to leave partner on lead to switch to a spade through the dummy. But any spade losers declarer has he will still have later.

Since you do not need to play a diamond immediately if partner has the ace and queen, the best defence is to let declarer make his own arrangements and remove the possibility of a club ruff in dummy by overtaking partner's queen of clubs with your king and switching to a small trump. Later you will gain the lead in a black suit when you can hope to find out how many clubs partner has. When he plays the ten on the second round he surely has three; now you simply play ace and another heart, thus killing any hopes declarer might have had, either of ruffing a club in the dummy or of establishing dummy's spades. If you thought partner had four clubs you would switch to a diamond, hoping to set up the ruff.

On the above layout, an immediate heart switch ensures a 500 penalty while any other defence permits a club ruff in the dummy and the penalty is reduced to 300. This would be an inadequate return since East/West have 25 points between them and can make three no-trumps.

Problem 3

North/South Game. Dealer South.

♠ 9532
♡ 643
◇ J1094
♣ A6

♠ AK
♡ AQ
◇ A87532
♣ 985

West	North	East	South
–	–	–	1◇
Pass	2◇	Pass	3NT
All Pass			

Knowing of a few scattered values and four-card diamond support opposite, you decide to have a go at three no-trumps. West leads the seven of hearts. Plan the play.

Solution 3

North/South Game. Dealer South.

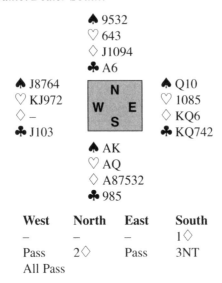

	♠ 9532	
	♡ 643	
	◇ J1094	
	♣ A6	

West	North	East	South
–	–	–	1◇
Pass	2◇	Pass	3NT
All Pass			

Knowing of a few scattered values and four-card diamond support opposite, you decide to have a go at three no-trumps. West leads the seven of hearts. Plan the play.

Having avoided a club lead, you have plenty of tricks provided you can bring in the diamond suit for only one loser. If the suit breaks 2-1 there is no problem, but what can you do about 3-0 breaks?

If West has three diamonds there is nothing to be done, but you must be careful to cater for East having the three-card diamond suit.

Win the heart lead and play a *low* diamond towards the dummy. If both opponents follow there are no further problems, but if West shows out you can later cross to dummy's ace of clubs to take a diamond finesse through East.

Problem 4

Game All. Dealer North.

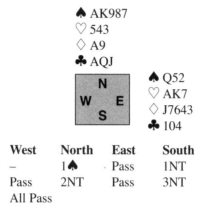

♠ AK987
♡ 543
◇ A9
♣ AQJ

♠ Q52
♡ AK7
◇ J7643
♣ 104

West	North	East	South
–	1♠	· Pass	1NT
Pass	2NT	Pass	3NT
All Pass			

Against South's three no-trumps, your partner leads the eight of hearts. You win with the king and declarer plays the two. Plan the defence.

Solution 4

Game All. Dealer North.

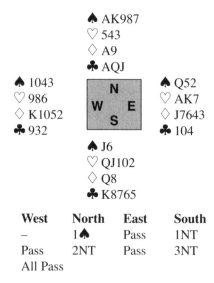

♠ AK987
♡ 543
◇ A9
♣ AQJ

♠ 1043
♡ 986
◇ K1052
♣ 932

♠ Q52
♡ AK7
◇ J7643
♣ 104

♠ J6
♡ QJ102
◇ Q8
♣ K8765

West	North	East	South
–	1♠	Pass	1NT
Pass	2NT	Pass	3NT
All Pass			

Against South's three no-trumps, your partner leads the eight of hearts. You win with the king and declarer plays the two. Plan the defence.

It looks very likely that declarer, given time, will make four spade tricks, one heart (presumably he has the queen and jack – the eight of hearts cannot be partner's fourth highest heart because that would give him QJ98, and from that holding he would have led the queen), one diamond and three clubs. It is possible declarer has a singleton spade so will make only three tricks in that suit; on the other hand he is likely to have more than three cards in either hearts or clubs which will provide extra tricks in those suits. So, if you blithely continue hearts declarer will probably make his contract.

Looking at that dummy, the only other possible source of tricks for your side is diamonds. So win the king of hearts and switch to the four of diamonds. Now there is no way declarer can make more than eight tricks.

Two further points of interest: look at the effectiveness of partner's opening lead. It often pays to try to find partner's suit when you have a weak hand and that, no doubt, was what partner was trying to do. Here it worked well for the wrong reason.

Also, note that declarer failed to make like more difficult for you by making a good falsecard. The one trouble with the style we have adopted in this book of leading second highest from bad holdings is that no-one has any idea of the length in the suit opened. Here declarer should have dropped a heart honour at trick one. This might have persuaded you that partner had five hearts to cash (depending on what he would lead from 108xxx).

Problem 5

East/West Game. Dealer South.

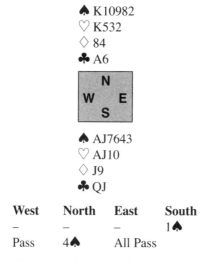

♠ K10982
♡ K532
◇ 84
♣ A6

♠ AJ7643
♡ AJ10
◇ J9
♣ QJ

West	North	East	South
–	–	–	1♠
Pass	4♠	All Pass	

West leads the ten of clubs against your four spades. Plan the play.

Solution 5

East/West Game. Dealer South.

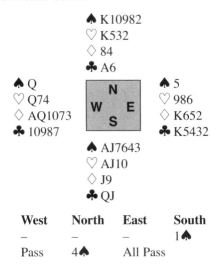

♠ K10982
♡ K532
◇ 84
♣ A6

♠ Q
♡ Q74
◇ AQ1073
♣ 10987

♠ 5
♡ 986
◇ K652
♣ K5432

♠ AJ7643
♡ AJ10
◇ J9
♣ QJ

West	North	East	South
–	–	–	1♠
Pass	4♠	All Pass	

West leads the ten of clubs against your four spades. Plan the play.

The obvious line of play is to finesse the club at trick one, hoping that West has led from the king. If East turns up with the king of clubs, then you must hope to guess who has the queen of hearts. Is there an improvement on this line?

Yes, there is a 100% line of play available, provided you spurn the club finesse at trick one. You must rise with the ace of clubs, draw trumps and exit with a club or a diamond. The defenders cannot do more than take one club and two diamonds before being forced either to broach the heart suit or to give a ruff and discard. If a defender is the first to lead a heart, then you must make three tricks in the suit. If a defender leads a third round of a minor suit, you discard your potential third-round heart loser from hand while ruffing in the dummy.

A big trump fit is a powerful advantage. It allows declarer to eliminate suits, draw trumps and throw the opponents in and still have enough trumps left to take advantage of a ruff and discard. It is not surprising that the Losing Trick Count method of hand evaluation deducts one loser for each card over four in the trump suit once it has been supported.

Problem 6

Game All. Dealer South.

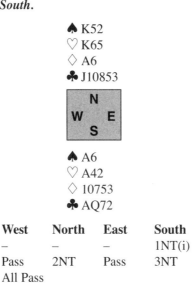

♠ K52
♡ K65
◇ A6
♣ J10853

♠ A6
♡ A42
◇ 10753
♣ AQ72

West	North	East	South
–	–	–	1NT(i)
Pass	2NT	Pass	3NT
All Pass			

(i) 12–14

West leads the four of diamonds against your three no-trumps. Plan the play.

Solution 6

Game All. Dealer South.

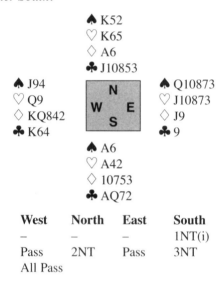

♠ K52
♡ K65
◇ A6
♣ J10853

♠ J94   ♠ Q10873
♡ Q9   ♡ J10873
◇ KQ842   ◇ J9
♣ K64   ♣ 9

♠ A6
♡ A42
◇ 10753
♣ AQ72

West	North	East	South
–	–	–	1NT(i)
Pass	2NT	Pass	3NT
All Pass			

(i) 12–14

West leads the four of diamonds against your three no-trumps. Plan the play.

There does not seem to be any shortage of tricks. In the fullness of time you should be able to make two spades, two hearts, one diamond and four clubs. The only danger is losing four diamonds as well as the king of clubs.

The main decision is whether or not to duck the opening lead. The important point to realise is that it is extremely unlikely that West holds all three top diamond honours. After all, if you held three touching top honours in a suit *after this sequence*, would you not lead an honour rather than a small card? If you duck at trick one, East will almost certainly win an honour and continue the suit. Then if West gets the lead with the king of clubs he may have three more diamonds to cash.

Now look at what happens if you rise with the ace of diamonds at trick one. If diamonds are 4-3 your contract is safe. If East has a doubleton honour he has no winning action. If he plays low, the suit is blocked; if he unblocks his top honour, West cannot continue the suit to advantage. Either way your contract is safe.

Problem 7

Game All. Dealer South.

♠ KJ1032
♡ 76
♢ KJ
♣ QJ76

♠ AQ
♡ A4
♢ A43
♣ K108432

West	North	East	South
–	–	–	1♣
Pass	1♠	Pass	2NT
Pass	3♣	Pass	3NT
All Pass			

West leads the queen of hearts against your three no-trumps. Plan the play.

Solution 7

Game All. Dealer South.

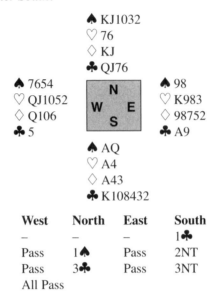

	♠ KJ1032	
	♡ 76	
	◇ KJ	
	♣ QJ76	

♠ 7654   ♠ 98
♡ QJ1052   ♡ K983
◇ Q106   ◇ 98752
♣ 5   ♣ A9

          ♠ AQ
          ♡ A4
          ◇ A43
          ♣ K108432

West	North	East	South
–	–	–	1♣
Pass	1♠	Pass	2NT
Pass	3♣	Pass	3NT
All Pass			

West leads the queen of hearts against your three no-trumps. Plan the play.

You have not done well in the bidding here. Three no-trumps is certainly a much worse contract than five clubs or four spades – if you play three no-trumps correctly, it actually has more or less the same chances of success as *six* clubs. Still, that is no reason to go down; everybody bids badly sometimes – the secret is to get away with it as often as possible.

If you make the straightforward play of holding up your ace of hearts for a round and then knocking out the ace of clubs, you will need a miracle heart blockage to make your contract. You have eight top tricks without resorting to the club suit: a much better chance for your ninth is to take the diamond finesse. However, you need to be careful with your entries.

Hold up your ace of hearts until the second round, then play a diamond to dummy's jack. When it holds, cash the king of diamonds, cross to your *ace* of spades and cash the ace of diamonds. Finally, overtake your queen of spades with dummy's king and run the spades: nine rather breathless tricks.

Problem 8

Love All. Dealer East.

This hand is presented as a two-part problem. First consider your play to trick two.

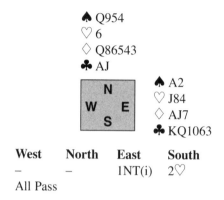

♠ Q954
♡ 6
◇ Q86543
♣ AJ

♠ A2
♡ J84
◇ AJ7
♣ KQ1063

West	North	East	South
–	–	1NT(i)	2♡
All Pass			

(i) 14–16

Your partner leads the four of clubs against two hearts. Declarer plays the jack from the dummy, which you win with the queen. What do you play now?

-o-o-o-o-o-

Because you have the aces of both spades and diamonds you should return a club. You know that declarer cannot get back to his hand to take a club ruff in the dummy and it is better to knock out his one dummy entry.

Declarer wins your club continuation with the ace in dummy and plays a low diamond. What now?

Solution 8

Love All. Dealer East.

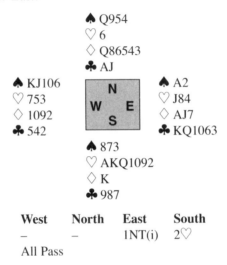

♠ Q954
♡ 6
◇ Q86543
♣ AJ

♠ KJ106
♡ 753
◇ 1092
♣ 542

♠ A2
♡ J84
◇ AJ7
♣ KQ1063

♠ 873
♡ AKQ1092
◇ K
♣ 987

West	North	East	South
–	–	1NT(i)	2♡
All Pass			

(i) 14–16

Your partner leads the four of clubs against two hearts. Declarer plays the jack from the dummy, which you win with the queen. What do you play now?

-o-o-o-o-o-

Because you have the aces of both spades and diamonds you should return a club. You know that declarer cannot get back to his hand to take a club ruff in the dummy and it is better to knock out his one entry to dummy.

Declarer wins your club continuation with the ace in dummy and plays a low diamond. What now?

It is generally safe to assume that if partner has a singleton in an unbid suit against a suit contract he will lead it (though the exceptions might be when he has either lots of trump tricks, or perhaps has nearly all the defensive strength). Here it is inconceivable that partner has a singleton diamond so declarer cannot have more than a doubleton. If he has a doubleton you can afford to rise with the ace for the suit is blocked. If he has a singleton, it will not matter what you do unless he has the singleton king. Rise with the ace of diamonds and play a trump.

When your side next gets the lead it will continue clubs. You do not yet know whether or not you are going to beat two hearts; it all depends on declarer's precise holdings in the majors, but you can be sure that you will take as many defensive tricks as possible. On the actual lie you will beat the contract.

It looks as if South's two heart bid was ill-chosen as the defence should manage to take six hearts, one diamond and one club against one no-trump. The trouble with passing one no-trump, however, is that it makes competition more difficult if West removes one no-trump, to two spades or three of a minor for instance.

Problem 9

North/South Game. Dealer South.

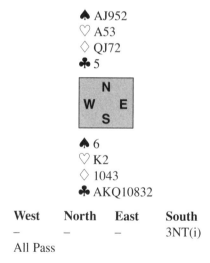

♠ AJ952
♡ A53
◇ QJ72
♣ 5

♠ 6
♡ K2
◇ 1043
♣ AKQ10832

West	North	East	South
–	–	–	3NT(i)
All Pass			

(i) gambling; long, good minor with no more than a king outside

West leads the ten of hearts against your three no-trumps. Plan the play.

Solution 9

North/South Game. Dealer South.

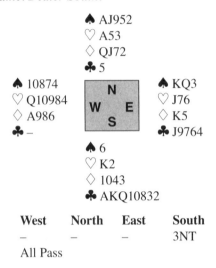

♠ AJ952
♡ A53
◇ QJ72
♣ 5

♠ 10874
♡ Q10984
◇ A986
♣ –

♠ KQ3
♡ J76
◇ K5
♣ J9764

♠ 6
♡ K2
◇ 1043
♣ AKQ10832

West	North	East	South
–	–	–	3NT
All Pass			

West leads the ten of hearts against your three no-trumps. Plan the play.

Win the heart lead in dummy and play a club to your ten. If it loses you can win the return and claim nine tricks. However, on this occasion West shows out and, feeling rather pleased with yourself, you clock up your vulnerable game.

This is a straightforward deal, easier to get right on paper than at the table. All you need for your contract is *six* club tricks, to go with one spade and two hearts. This will not be a problem if clubs are 4-1 or better, so you need to concentrate on 5-0 breaks. If West has the five-card suit there is nothing you can do, but if it is East...

Note that South's three no-trump opening was slightly unsound at the given vulnerability. The suit isn't quite solid and if partner has to remove to Four Clubs there is a danger of conceding a substantial penalty.

Problem 10

East/West Game. Dealer East.

♠ J643
♡ K83
♢ 6
♣ J10842

West	North	East	South
–	–	2♢(i)	4♠
Pass	5♣	Pass	5♢
Pass	5♠	All Pass	

(i) weak

What would you lead from the West hand against South's contract of five spades?

Solution 10

East/West Game. Dealer East.

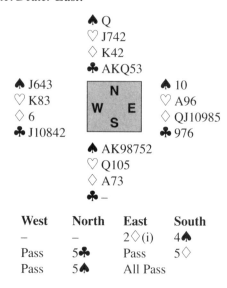

♠ Q
♡ J742
◇ K42
♣ AKQ53

♠ J643   ♠ 10
♡ K83   ♡ A96
◇ 6   ◇ QJ10985
♣ J10842   ♣ 976

♠ AK98752
♡ Q105
◇ A73
♣ –

West	North	East	South
–	–	2◇(i)	4♠
Pass	5♣	Pass	5◇
Pass	5♠	All Pass	

(i) weak

What would you lead from the West hand against South's contract of five spades?

You would not normally look further than a singleton in partner's suit, but here that would surely be the wrong thing to do. North has made a slam try of five clubs, but signed off in five spades after his partner's co-operative cue-bid of five diamonds. North cannot have a heart control, and if South had a heart control he would have bid on over the five spade sign-off.

On this auction, your side surely has the ace and king of hearts to cash, along with a more or less certain spade trick. The next thing to decide is whether to lead a low heart or the king. Leading a low heart risks partner thinking you have a void in diamonds, while leading the king is better as it gives him no chance to go wrong.

This deal happened at the table in the 1999 Cavendish tournament. North/South were Ron Smith and Billy Cohen. They were well in contention for the quarter of a million dollar first prize when this deal cropped up. West was the USA's top woman player, Kerri Sanborn. She found the heart lead which cost Smith/Cohen the title and dropped them down to third place.

Problem 11

Game All. Dealer North.

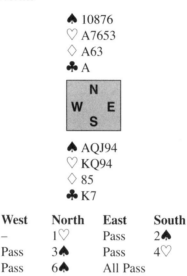

♠ 10876
♡ A7653
◇ A63
♣ A

♠ AQJ94
♡ KQ94
◇ 85
♣ K7

West	North	East	South
–	1♡	Pass	2♠
Pass	3♠	Pass	4♡
Pass	6♠	All Pass	

A good sequence to the fair slam. Over your four hearts, North had to go on with his three aces and there was not much point in using Blackwood. The simple jump to slam was best. It is a pity the minor suits didn't fit better but you can't have it all.

West leads the king of diamonds. Obviously the spade finesse needs to be right or you are down in top tricks. Can you foresee any other problems?

Solution 11

Game All. Dealer North.

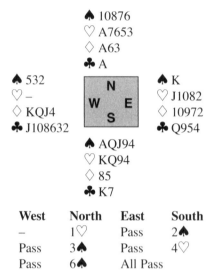

♠ 10876
♡ A7653
◇ A63
♣ A

♠ 532
♡ –
◇ KQJ4
♣ J108632

♠ K
♡ J1082
◇ 10972
♣ Q954

♠ AQJ94
♡ KQ94
◇ 85
♣ K7

West	North	East	South
–	1♡	Pass	2♠
Pass	3♠	Pass	4♡
Pass	6♠	All Pass	

West leads the king of diamonds. Obviously the spade finesse needs to be right or you are down in top tricks. Can you foresee any other problems?

If the spade finesse is right, you will succeed unless hearts break 4-0. If hearts do break 4-0, you can pick the suit up for no loser only if it is East who has the four-card holding.

The correct sequence of plays is: win the ace of diamonds, play the eight of spades from dummy (if you start with the ten and East has four you cannot draw all the trumps immediately) and win East's king with your ace. Draw the rest of the trumps, then play a heart to dummy's ace. When West shows out, you play a heart back to East's ten and your queen. Now cross to the ace of clubs and take a marked finesse of East's jack of hearts. Cash your other heart winner. Cross to dummy either with a trump or by ruffing your king of clubs, and cash your long heart discarding your diamond loser. You have made an overtrick.

Problem 12

Game All. Dealer West.

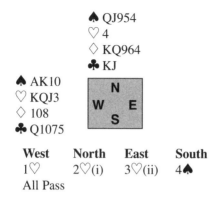

♠ QJ954
♡ 4
◇ KQ964
♣ KJ

♠ AK10
♡ KQJ3
◇ 108
♣ Q1075

West	North	East	South
1♡	2♡(i)	3♡(ii)	4♠
All Pass			

(i) Michaels cue-bid, showing five spades and five cards in a minor
(ii) with a full-value limit raise, East would cue-bid two spades, so three hearts here is weaker than without intervention

Against South's four spades you lead the king of hearts. This holds the trick, partner playing the eight. Plan the defence.

Solution 12

Game All. Dealer West.

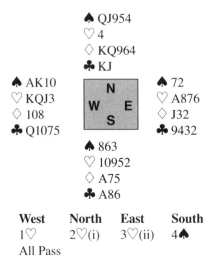

♠ QJ954
♡ 4
◇ KQ964
♣ KJ

♠ AK10
♡ KQJ3
◇ 108
♣ Q1075

♠ 72
♡ A876
◇ J32
♣ 9432

♠ 863
♡ 10952
◇ A75
♣ A86

West	North	East	South
1♡	2♡(i)	3♡(ii)	4♠
All Pass			

(i) Michaels cue-bid, showing five spades and five cards in a minor
(ii) with a full-value limit raise, East would cue-bid two spades, so three hearts here is weaker than without intervention

Against South's four spades you lead the king of hearts. This holds the trick, partner playing the eight. Plan the defence.

Assuming partner has four hearts to the ace (a virtual certainty) you can see how to beat four spades in your own hand. All you must do is continue hearts at every opportunity. At trick two declarer ruffs in dummy, then, say, he reaches his hand with a minor-suit ace and plays a trump. You go in with the king and play a third heart. He must ruff again and that reduces dummy's trump holding to just queen-jack doubleton. When you get in with your ace of trumps you can play a fourth heart which he must ruff with one of his honours, thus promoting your ten into a certain trick.

The occasions when you can see the demise of a contract with no help at all from partner are rare, but be on the look out for them, for once you have seen how to defend, at least nothing can go wrong.

Problem 13

Game All. Dealer West.

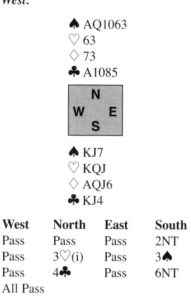

♠ AQ1063
♡ 63
◇ 73
♣ A1085

♠ KJ7
♡ KQJ
◇ AQJ6
♣ KJ4

West	North	East	South
Pass	Pass	Pass	2NT
Pass	3♡(i)	Pass	3♠
Pass	4♣	Pass	6NT
All Pass			

(i) transfer to spades

In the bidding North's three hearts is a transfer to spades; then four clubs shows a second suit with slam interest. South's fitting cards in the black suits persuades him to jump to the no-trump slam.

Against your six no-trumps West leads the ace of hearts and continues with another heart. Plan the play.

Solution 13

Game All. Dealer West.

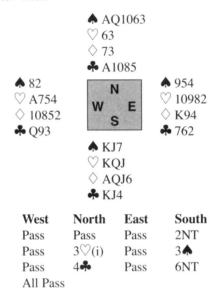

♠ AQ1063
♡ 63
◇ 73
♣ A1085

♠ 82
♡ A754
◇ 10852
♣ Q93

♠ 954
♡ 10982
◇ K94
♣ 762

♠ KJ7
♡ KQJ
◇ AQJ6
♣ KJ4

West	North	East	South
Pass	Pass	Pass	2NT
Pass	3♡(i)	Pass	3♠
Pass	4♣	Pass	6NT
All Pass			

(i) transfer to spades

Against your six no-trumps West leads the ace of hearts and continues with another heart. Plan the play.

There are ten tricks on top: five spades, two hearts, one diamond and two clubs. There are two possibilities for the extra tricks: either the diamond finesse or a successful guess as to who has the queen of clubs. In this type of situation you should look for a line of play which combines these chances to as great a degree as possible.

Declarer should cash the ace and king of clubs to see if the queen drops; then, if it does not, he should take a diamond finesse.

It is often a good idea to run your long suit first, in order to force the defenders to make several, hopefully revealing, discards. So, should you start by running your spades? No, because then you will not have the entries needed to take two diamond finesses.

This is the correct sequence of plays. Win the heart at trick two. Cash the king of clubs followed by the ace of clubs. If the queen drops, claim; if the queen does not drop take a diamond finesse. Then cash your spades, discarding a diamond and a club from your hand before taking a second diamond finesse for your contract.

Problem 14

East/West Game. Dealer East.

You, South, hold:

♠ J75
♡ K
♦ AJ974
♣ QJ82

What do you bid after the following sequence:

West	North	East	South
–	–	Pass	1♦
Pass	1♠	Pass	2♣
Pass	3♦	Pass	?

Solution 14

East/West Game. Dealer East.

You, South, hold:

♠ J75
♡ K
♢ AJ974
♣ QJ82

What do you bid after the following sequence:

West	North	East	South
–	–	Pass	1♢
Pass	1♠	Pass	2♠
Pass	3♢	Pass	?

Although it is tempting to pass because you have a (sub-)minimum opening and only three-card support for spades, partner's three diamonds must be forcing. If he did not have a strong hand he would not try to play in a minor-suit when he had already found a major-suit fit. With an invitational hand and only four spades he would have bid two no-trumps. So, what is the most descriptive bid you can make?

The one bid you should not make is three spades. One of the more likely reasons for partner's three diamonds is to discover whether or not you have four-card spade support. If you bid three spades he will think you have four spades and not look beyond that suit as a final denomination.

Think about what types of hand you could have. If you had a balanced hand in the 12–14 range you would have opened one no-trump; if you were balanced with 15+ you would not have raised spades (rather than rebid no-trumps) unless you had four-card spade support, when you would bid four spades now. What is left are unbalanced hands. With 15 or more points and four spades you would have jump raised; with three spades you would have introduced your other four-card suit. With 12–14 points and four-card spade support you would bid three (or four) spades now, hence all other bids must show 12–14 HCP in an unbalanced hand without four spades.

Having said all that, the most descriptive bid on your hand is surely three no-trumps as half your points are in the unbid suits. Partner will of course convert to four spades if he has five. As you will see from the full deal, four spades is high enough, but six diamonds can be made with careful play.

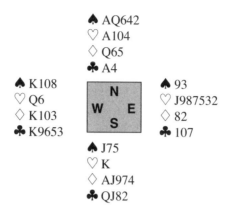

At the table, North was not pleased when South passed three diamonds! When in doubt about a bidding situation it is foolish to pass and risk missing a game or slam; if you bid on, the worst that can happen is to go one down instead of making a partscore.

Problem 15

Love All. Dealer South.

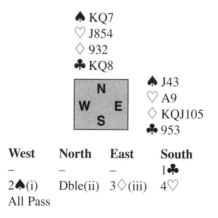

West	North	East	South
–	–	–	1♣
2♠(i)	Dble(ii)	3◇(iii)	4♡
All Pass			

(i) weak (ii) negative, with 4 hearts (iii) spade raise with diamond values

Against South's four hearts, West leads the eight of diamonds. Your ten wins the first trick. Plan the defence.

Solution 15

Love All. Dealer South.

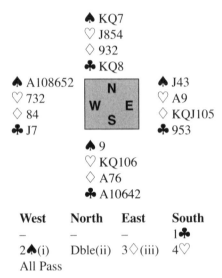

♠ KQ7
♡ J854
◇ 932
♣ KQ8

♠ A108652
♡ 732
◇ 84
♣ J7

♠ J43
♡ A9
◇ KQJ105
♣ 953

♠ 9
♡ KQ106
◇ A76
♣ A10642

West	North	East	South
–	–	–	1♣
2♠(i)	Dble(ii)	3◇(iii)	4♡
All Pass			

(i) weak (ii) negative, with 4 hearts (iii) spade raise with diamond values

Against South's four hearts, West leads the eight of diamonds. Your ten wins the first trick. Plan the defence.

Assuming your partner has ace to six spades and a doubleton diamond you can see that four hearts should go down. All you have to do is continue diamonds to declarer's ace. If he tries to draw trumps you will win and then cash your diamond trick followed by partner's spade. Declarer cannot take any discards on his clubs for your partner will ruff in quickly enough. The only chance for declarer is to try a spade at trick three. Your partner will win his ace but then needs to find your entry quickly. You must try to help him switch to a heart rather than a club.

At trick two play the *king* of diamonds. This is a suit-preference position, so by playing the king (rather than the queen or jack which you are known to hold) you are certainly not asking him to play a club. You can reinforce this message by playing the jack of spades when partner takes his ace since you would hardly support him at the three level with a singleton.

When you first learn about suit-preference signals it is in the context of playing a suit for partner to ruff. If you play a high card you want partner to return the higher non-trump suit; if you return a low card you want him to return the lower suit. However, there are plenty more opportunities to use suit-preference signals. Here, the order in which you play your high cards, once your holding is known, can be used to express suit-preference.

In some other situations you can help partner by the order in which you play your small cards. Say you have 952 in a suit. On the first round you play the two to show an odd number, but on the second round you have a free choice between the nine and the five. Play the nine with a strong holding in the higher-ranking suit, otherwise play the five. Such methods would have prevented the game swing above which occurred in the 1955 Bermuda Bowl.

Problem 16

Game All. Dealer East.

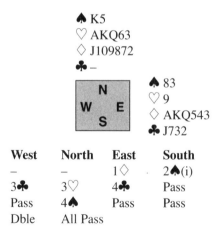

```
                ♠ K5
                ♡ AKQ63
                ◇ J109872
                ♣ –
              ┌─────────┐    ♠ 83
              │   N     │    ♡ 9
              │ W     E │    ◇ AKQ543
              │   S     │    ♣ J732
              └─────────┘
```

West	North	East	South
–	–	1◇	2♠(i)
3♣	3♡	4♣	Pass
Pass	4♠	Pass	Pass
Dble	All Pass		

(i) weak

Against the doubled game West leads the king of clubs, ruffed low in dummy by declarer who tries the ace of hearts from the dummy (your partner playing the four). Declarer follows with the king of hearts. Over to you...

Solution 16

Game All. Dealer East.

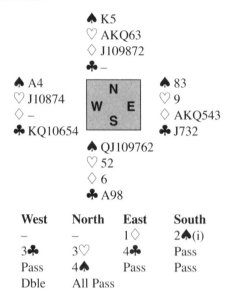

♠ K5
♡ AKQ63
◇ J109872
♣ —

♠ A4
♡ J10874
◇ —
♣ KQ10654

♠ 83
♡ 9
◇ AKQ543
♣ J732

♠ QJ109762
♡ 52
◇ 6
♣ A98

West	North	East	South
–	–	1◇	2♠(i)
3♣	3♡	4♣	Pass
Pass	4♠	Pass	Pass
Dble	All Pass		

(i) weak

Against the doubled game West leads the king of clubs, ruffed low in dummy by declarer who tries the ace of hearts from the dummy (your partner playing the four). Declarer follows with the king of hearts. Over to you...

There certainly seems no reason to refuse to ruff the king of hearts with your low trump. But what are you going to do next?

Either declarer or your partner clearly has a void in diamonds and there are several reasons to suppose it is your partner: firstly, he would probably have led a singleton diamond had he held one, and secondly, if declarer had a void diamond he should have ruffed a diamond to his hand and ruffed a second club before trying to cash his heart winners.

So is it clear to play a top diamond? And if so what next? Another diamond to promote a trump trick for West, or a trump? Partner's double gives the clue. He surely has the ace of spades, in which case we will make a spade and a club to defeat the contract by one trick. Since partner has no problem with exit cards and declarer has no entry to dummy it is better to play a spade before the ace of diamonds just in case declarer is void after all. If it doesn't cost to cater for all eventualities, then do so.

Declarer rather mangled this hand. He should, of course, ruff the club lead high and play a trump, threatening to make six spades in hand, one ruff in dummy, the ace of clubs and three heart tricks. However, if he does this, your partner will win the ace of spades and play a heart. If declarer plays a diamond, West will ruff and play another heart for you to ruff. Eventually you will make a club for down one.

Problem 17

Game All. Dealer East

♠ K983
♡ KQJ109
♢ A103
♣ 7

♠ J104
♡ 7632
♢ K95
♣ A65

West	North	East	South
–	–	1NT(i)	Pass
Pass	2♣(ii)	Pass	2♡
3♣	3♡	Pass	4♡
All Pass			

(i) 12–14 (ii) majors

Against your four hearts West leads the four of clubs to dummy's seven and East's queen. Plan the play.

Solution 17

Game All. Dealer East

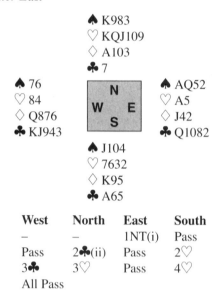

```
                    ♠ K983
                    ♡ KQJ109
                    ◇ A103
                    ♣ 7
    ♠ 76                           ♠ AQ52
    ♡ 84              N            ♡ A5
    ◇ Q876        W     E          ◇ J42
    ♣ KJ943          S             ♣ Q1082
                    ♠ J104
                    ♡ 7632
                    ◇ K95
                    ♣ A65
```

West	North	East	South
–	–	1NT(i)	Pass
Pass	2♣(ii)	Pass	2♡
3♣	3♡	Pass	4♡
All Pass			

(i) 12–14 (ii) majors

Against your four hearts West leads the four of clubs to dummy's seven and East's queen. Plan the play.

At the table, South reasoned that he had a loser in spades, hearts and diamonds and that he needed West to hold the queen of spades. With a general shortage of entries to his hand he won the ace of clubs at trick one and led the jack of spades. Unfortunately for him, East won the queen, cashed the ace and gave his partner a spade ruff to beat the contract by one.

Declarer's count of his losers was at fault here. Every time the diamond honours are split the defenders cannot establish a diamond trick before declarer establishes a spade trick for a diamond discard.

Declarer should simply win the ace of clubs and play a heart. Say East wins and continues clubs. Declarer ruffs in dummy, draws trumps and plays a spade. East wins his queen but there is nothing he can do.

Can you see where the defence had a chance to persuade declarer to go wrong? When East is in with the ace of hearts he should switch to the jack of diamonds. Declarer now has to guess whether he has switched from the jack alone or from the queen-jack.

Problem 18

Love All. Dealer North.

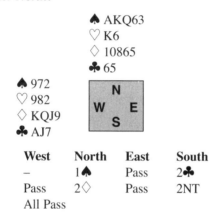

♠ AKQ63
♡ K6
◇ 10865
♣ 65

♠ 972
♡ 982
◇ KQJ9
♣ AJ7

West	North	East	South
–	1♠	Pass	2♣
Pass	2◇	Pass	2NT
All Pass			

Against South's two no-trumps, you lead the king of diamonds. Declarer wins with the ace and returns a diamond to your jack. Partner plays high-low to show an even number. Plan the defence.

Solution 18

Love All. Dealer North.

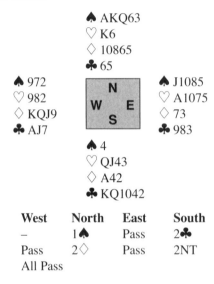

♠ AKQ63
♡ K6
◇ 10865
♣ 65

♠ 972
♡ 982
◇ KQJ9
♣ AJ7

♠ J1085
♡ A1075
◇ 73
♣ 983

♠ 4
♡ QJ43
◇ A42
♣ KQ1042

West	North	East	South
–	1♠	Pass	2♣
Pass	2◇	Pass	2NT
All Pass			

Against South's two no-trumps, you lead the king of diamonds. Declarer wins with the ace and returns a diamond to your jack. Partner plays high-low to show an even number. Plan the defence.

This is a fairly common sort of defensive problem which is often not solved by average players. The first thing to realise is that it is virtually impossible to imagine that you can take the next five tricks. Declarer is not threatening to establish a great number of tricks anywhere, so your priority is to try to disrupt his communications.

The best switch at this stage is a spade. If declarer has a doubleton spade he is certain to make two no-trumps because he has five spade tricks. If that is the case you can be sure that he will test the suit before trying an alternative line that could go down. However, if declarer has only a singleton spade, it is in the defence's interests to attack the suit now, to force him to take his winners there as soon as possible. Also, the spades are entries to what will soon be an established diamond.

Work through the play, first on a spade switch, and then on a heart, which does not seem to give anything away. You will see that on a spade switch, however many spade tricks declarer decides to take, he cannot succeed. If you switch to a heart, on the other hand, declarer plays low from dummy. Your partner cannot win the ace without squandering a heart trick. Declarer wins in hand and plays a third diamond. In time he must come to three spades, two hearts, two diamonds and a club – you can never make more than one spade, one heart, two diamonds and a club.

Problem 19

North/South Game. Dealer North.

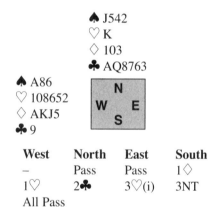

	♠ J542		
	♡ K		
	◇ 103		
	♣ AQ8763		

♠ A86
♡ 108652
◇ AKJ5
♣ 9

West	North	East	South
–	Pass	Pass	1◇
1♡	2♣	3♡(i)	3NT
All Pass			

(i) pre-emptive

Against South's three no-trumps you lead the five of hearts and dummy's king holds. Partner plays the seven, an encouraging card when dummy's singleton honour card is going to win the trick. At trick two, declarer plays a spade to his king (partner playing the three). Over to you.

Solution 19

North/South Game. Dealer North.

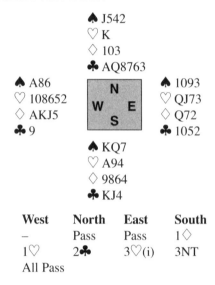

♠ J542
♡ K
◇ 103
♣ AQ8763

♠ A86
♡ 108652
◇ AKJ5
♣ 9

♠ 1093
♡ QJ73
◇ Q72
♣ 1052

♠ KQ7
♡ A94
◇ 9864
♣ KJ4

West	North	East	South
–	Pass	Pass	1◇
1♡	2♣	3♡(i)	3NT
All Pass			

(i) pre-emptive

Against South's three no-trumps you lead the five of hearts and dummy's king holds. Partner plays the seven, an encouraging card when dummy's singleton honour card is going to win the trick. At trick two, declarer plays a spade to his king (partner playing the three). Over to you.

The first thing to realise is that there is a very real chance that declarer will have nine tricks if you duck this trick. He clearly has little more than a minimum opening bid for his three no-trump call, so it is likely that he has bid on the strength of a club fit. If the club suit is running, he has six clubs, two hearts and the king of spades.

So, you must win your ace of spades. If partner has the queen of diamonds or queen of spades you can beat three no-trumps. Which is your best chance? It looks from the play to the first two tricks as if declarer is 3-3 in the majors. If the club suit is to be running he must have three clubs. Therefore you can afford to play partner for three diamonds. If this is the case you should start by playing the ace of diamonds to get an attitude signal from partner. On his actual hand partner will play the seven of diamonds to encourage the suit. You will then play a diamond to his queen and he will have a third diamond to play back to your hand. With the queen of spades instead of the queen of diamonds (leading up to his king of spades may have been declarer's only chance), he would have discouraged diamonds (with the two) and you would have returned a spade. Then a diamond through declarer's queen would have meant you could take two more diamond tricks.

Note that this is not foolproof. Partner could have started out with 987 of diamonds, in which case his seven would have been intended as discouraging. All you can do is go with the odds.

Problem 20

North/South Game. Dealer North.

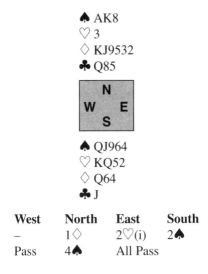

♠ AK8
♡ 3
◇ KJ9532
♣ Q85

♠ QJ964
♡ KQ52
◇ Q64
♣ J

West	North	East	South
–	1◇	2♡(i)	2♠
Pass	4♠	All Pass	

(i) weak

Against your four spades, West leads the ace of hearts and continues with a second heart. What is your best line of play?

Solution 20

North/South Game. Dealer North.

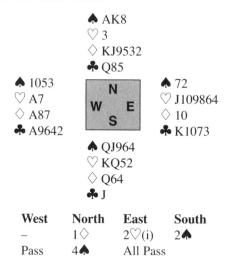

♠ AK8
♥ 3
♦ KJ9532
♣ Q85

♠ 1053
♥ A7
♦ A87
♣ A9642

♠ 72
♥ J109864
♦ 10
♣ K1073

♠ QJ964
♥ KQ52
♦ Q64
♣ J

West	North	East	South
–	1◇	2♡(i)	2♠
Pass	4♠	All Pass	

(i) weak

Against your four spades, West leads the ace of hearts and continues with a second heart. What is your best line of play?

There are three possible alternatives. First, you could ruff low, cash the ace and king of spades and play a club to your hand. However, this is very unlikely to succeed because either West will be able to get a heart ruff or East a diamond ruff (only if West is precisely 2-2-2-7 will this line work). Second, you could win the heart in your hand, draw trumps and play diamonds. This would work if diamonds were 2-2 or the ace was singleton. However, whenever diamonds are 3-1, the defenders would simply hold off their ace until the third round and you would have inevitable losers in both hearts and clubs. Third, you could ruff high and draw trumps, hoping they break or the ten drops. If so, then you are home once you have knocked out the ace of diamonds.

A 3-2 spade break itself is nearly 68% while a 2-2 diamond break is only just over 40%, so line three is the best percentage chance and works this time.

PART TWO

Problem 21

Love All. Dealer East.

♠ 103
♡ KQ4
◇ A954
♣ 10972

♠ A75
♡ AJ95
◇ 83
♣ AKJ6

West	North	East	South
–	–	Pass	1♡
1♠	Dble(i)	Pass	2NT
Pass	3♡	Pass	3NT
All Pass			

(i) negative

Against your three no-trumps, West leads the king of spades on which East plays the four. You hold up and West continues with the queen of spades, East playing the two this time. Over to you.

Solution 21

Love All. Dealer East.

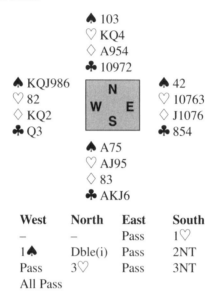

♠ 103
♡ KQ4
◇ A954
♣ 10972

♠ KQJ986
♡ 82
◇ KQ2
♣ Q3

♠ 42
♡ 10763
◇ J1076
♣ 854

♠ A75
♡ AJ95
◇ 83
♣ AKJ6

West	North	East	South
–	–	Pass	1♡
1♠	Dble(i)	Pass	2NT
Pass	3♡	Pass	3NT
All Pass			

(i) negative

Against your three no-trumps, West leads the king of spades on which East plays the four. You hold up and West continues with the queen of spades, East playing the two this time. Over to you.

You should not have any problem arriving at nine tricks since you have one spade, four hearts, one diamond and three clubs (though you may first have to lose to the queen). Your problem here is one of losers. If you finesse a club to West and he has the queen he has an awful lot of spades to cash.

At the table, the successful declarer won the second spade, because he had trusted East's high-low signal, showing an even number of cards. He then cashed four rounds of hearts, just in case anyone discarded clubs. He followed this by cashing the ace and king of clubs, thus making sure he did not lose a club trick to the West hand unless it was absolutely necessary. When West's queen dropped he quickly claimed ten tricks.

Maybe you are thinking that winning the second spade was unnecessary and that it would have been safer for declarer to duck again. That is what happened in the other room and West brightly switched to the king of diamonds at trick three. Declarer was now feeling distinctly unhappy. He ducked the king of diamonds and West continued the suit. At the first table declarer had identified West as the danger hand and it was right to lay down the top clubs in order to try to avoid losing a club to him. At this table there was no danger hand. If he lost a club trick to East, East would be able to cash diamond tricks. Consequently declarer took his best shot in the club suit, by first cashing the ace and then crossing to dummy to finesse the jack. West won his queen and played a diamond for East to cash two tricks in the suit and take three no-trumps two down.

Problem 22

East/West Game. Dealer South.

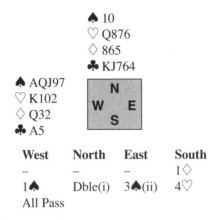

♠ 10
♡ Q876
♢ 865
♣ KJ764

♠ AQJ97
♡ K102
♢ Q32
♣ A5

West	North	East	South
–	–	–	1♢
1♠	Dble(i)	3♠(ii)	4♡
All Pass			

(i) negative   (ii) pre-emptive

You fancied your defensive prospects against Four Hearts and perhaps you should have doubled. You certainly didn't consider going on to Four Spades.

You lead the ace of spades on which your partner plays the six and declarer the four. With a singleton spade in the dummy you would expect your partner to give you a suit-preference signal, but the six is unlikely to be his highest or his lowest card. Plan the defence.

Solution 22

East/West Game. Dealer South.

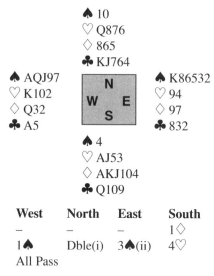

♠ 10
♡ Q876
◇ 865
♣ KJ764

♠ AQJ97
♡ K102
◇ Q32
♣ A5

♠ K86532
♡ 94
◇ 97
♣ 832

♠ 4
♡ AJ53
◇ AKJ104
♣ Q109

West	North	East	South
–	–	–	1◇
1♠	Dble(i)	3♠(ii)	4♡
All Pass			

(i) negative (ii) pre-emptive

You lead the ace of spades on which your partner plays the six and declarer the four. With a singleton spade in the dummy you would expect your partner to give you a suit-preference signal, but the six is unlikely to be his highest or his lowest card. Plan the defence.

Assuming your partner has the king of spades, he is unlikely to have much else in the way of high cards for South to have his bid. If that is the case, he must have a lot of spades for his pre-emptive three spade bid at adverse vulnerability. If declarer's distribution is 1-4-5-3, quite likely on the bidding, you must be careful to preserve the four defensive tricks you can see.

The only defence guaranteed to beat four hearts is to play ace and another club at tricks two and three. You then sit back and wait for your queen of diamonds and king of hearts.

At the table, West played a low heart at trick two. Declarer won cheaply and played a club. West rose with the ace and exited with a club but declarer read the hand well. He cashed the ace of hearts and played a club in case West had three. When West refused to ruff declarer exited with a heart. Now West had to give declarer a ruff and discard or broach the diamond suit.

Problem 23

Love All. Dealer South.

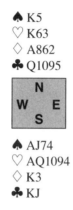

♠ K5
♡ K63
◇ A862
♣ Q1095

♠ AJ74
♡ AQ1094
◇ K3
♣ KJ

West	North	East	South
–	–	–	1♡
1♠	Dble(i)	Pass	2NT
Pass	3♡	Pass	3♠(ii)
Pass	4◇(ii)	Pass	4♡
Pass	4♠(ii)	Pass	6♡
All Pass			

(i) negative or Sputnik
(ii) cue-bids

Some spirited North/South bidding led to the good slam. West leads the queen of diamonds. Can you see any problems?

Solution 23

Love All. Dealer South.

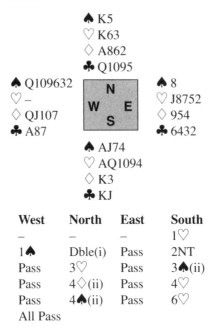

	♠ K5	
	♡ K63	
	◇ A862	
	♣ Q1095	

♠ Q109632
♡ –
◇ QJ107
♣ A87

♠ 8
♡ J8752
◇ 954
♣ 6432

♠ AJ74
♡ AQ1094
◇ K3
♣ KJ

West	North	East	South
–	–	–	1♡
1♠	Dble(i)	Pass	2NT
Pass	3♡	Pass	3♠(ii)
Pass	4◇(ii)	Pass	4♡
Pass	4♠(ii)	Pass	6♡
All Pass			

(i) negative or Sputnik
(ii) cue-bids

Some spirited North/South bidding led to the good slam. West leads the queen of diamonds. Can you see any problems?

If you count your tricks you will see that you have twelve provided you can count on five heart tricks: two spades, five hearts, two diamonds and three clubs (once you have knocked out the ace). What can go wrong?

You need to make sure you do not lose a heart trick. If East has Jxxx you can pick up the suit for no loser without a problem, but if West has Jxxx (less likely anyway, on the bidding) you will never guess to pick up his holding. You can also succeed if East has all five hearts but you must be sure to cash the king first.

Win the king of diamonds in hand and play a heart to dummy's king. West does indeed show out. Now play a heart to your ten. How should you get back to dummy. You have to lose the lead later in the hand after you have exhausted everyone of trumps so you cannot afford to leave a suit unstopped. So, cross back to the king of spades and take another heart finesse. Now you can draw trumps, discarding two diamonds from the dummy. The next thing to do is to knock out the ace of clubs, after which you can claim your twelve tricks.

Problem 24

Love All. Dealer South.

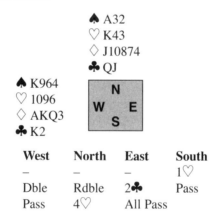

♠ A32
♡ K43
◇ J10874
♣ QJ

♠ K964
♡ 1096
◇ AKQ3
♣ K2

West	North	East	South
–	–	–	1♡
Dble	Rdble	2♣	Pass
Pass	4♡	All Pass	

Against four hearts you lead the ace of diamonds and your partner plays the nine. You notice that dummy has made a wild overbid but even so there is little chance of partner having many values. Plan the defence.

Solution 24

Love All. Dealer South.

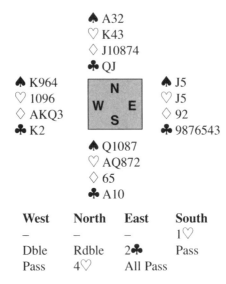

                    ♠ A32
                    ♡ K43
                    ◇ J10874
                    ♣ QJ
    ♠ K964   ♠ J5
    ♡ 1096   ♡ J5
    ◇ AKQ3   ◇ 92
    ♣ K2   ♣ 9876543
                    ♠ Q1087
                    ♡ AQ872
                    ◇ 65
                    ♣ A10

West	North	East	South
–	–	–	1♡
Dble	Rdble	2♣	Pass
Pass	4♡	All Pass	

Against four hearts you lead the ace of diamonds and your partner plays the nine. You notice that dummy has made a wild overbid but even so there is little chance of partner having many values. Plan the defence.

It looks as though both your partner and declarer have doubleton diamonds so you can count on two tricks in that suit. If declarer is 3-5-2-3 or 4-5-2-2 he is threatening to draw trumps and give you two more diamond tricks. Your only safe exit will be a small diamond which declarer will win in dummy to cash his diamonds. Declarer will have discarded two spades and a club as he plays dummy's diamonds. When he crosses to the ace of clubs to play two more trumps you will be squeezed in the black suits. What can you do?

Although it is unlikely that partner can contribute much in the way of high cards, there is just room for him to hold a couple of useful jacks. If he has the jack of hearts you can promote a trump trick for yourself.

Cash the king of diamonds and at trick three continue with the three of diamonds. Partner should ruff this as high as he can. If he has the jack that will promote you a trump trick; if he does not then you have not lost anything. As the cards lie, after this defence you cannot help but beat the game.

This hand occurred in the European Bridge League Senior Pairs, though the bidding would have seemed more at home in a junior event!, West switched to a trump at trick three. The play continued as above with West squeezed in the black suits.

Problem 25

Game All. Dealer South.

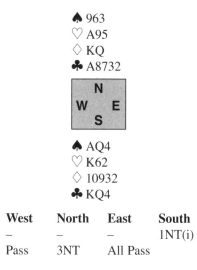

♠ 963
♡ A95
◇ KQ
♣ A8732

♠ AQ4
♡ K62
◇ 10932
♣ KQ4

West	North	East	South
–	–	–	1NT(i)
Pass	3NT	All Pass	

(i) 12–14

Against your three no-trumps, West leads the five of spades and East plays the king. Plan the play.

Solution 25

Game All. Dealer South.

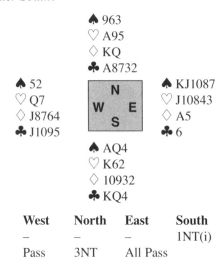

```
                    ♠ 963
                    ♡ A95
                    ◇ KQ
                    ♣ A8732
   ♠ 52                              ♠ KJ1087
   ♡ Q7          N                   ♡ J10843
   ◇ J8764    W     E                ◇ A5
   ♣ J1095       S                   ♣ 6
                    ♠ AQ4
                    ♡ K62
                    ◇ 10932
                    ♣ KQ4
```

West	North	East	South
–	–	–	1NT(i)
Pass	3NT	All Pass	

(i) 12–14

Against your three no-trumps, West leads the five of spades and East plays the king. Plan the play.

A careless and optimistic count of your tricks would lead to nine, but clubs don't break 3-2 all the time. If that suit breaks 4-1 you will need to knock out the ace of diamonds in order to arrive at your nine tricks; then you have a choice between establishing an extra club or a diamond trick.

Clearly if someone has five spades and all the entries the contract is doomed. It isn't obvious who might have five spades; since dummy has shown no interest in the majors, West is likely to prefer a short suit in a major to a long poor suit in a minor.

If you win the ace of spades you will have to guess to knock out the entry held by the five-card suit. A much better play is to attack your opponents' communications by ducking the first trick.

If East continues spades, there is time to knock out both minor-suit stoppers. Best defence is for him to switch to a heart, but you should duck that as well. You win the heart continuation in hand and play a diamond. Say West wins and continues hearts. Win dummy's ace and test the clubs by cashing the king and queen. When you discover that West has long clubs and no more hearts you can safely lose a club trick to him. If East had had the long clubs you would have cashed the other top diamond, crossed to hand with a spade and played the ten of diamonds to establish a trick in that suit. A good hand for combining all your chances. If hearts are 4-3 you will be back to a guess as to who has four, but at least you've done your best.

Did you notice East's misdefence? He can tell from the spot cards that his partner has made a short-suit lead. Had he played the ten of spades at trick one it would have been almost impossible for you to duck. Mind you, declarer can still succeed by playing on diamonds.

Problem 26

Love All. Dealer South.

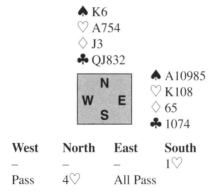

♠ K6
♡ A754
◇ J3
♣ QJ832

♠ A10985
♡ K108
◇ 65
♣ 1074

West	North	East	South
–	–	–	1♡
Pass	4♡	All Pass	

Your partner, West, leads the king of diamonds against South's four hearts. Declarer wins with the ace in hand and plays a heart to dummy's ace (your partner playing the jack) followed by another heart. Plan the defence.

Solution 26

Love All. Dealer South.

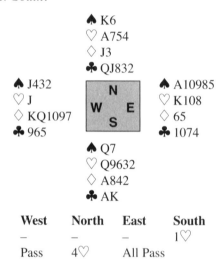

♠ K6
♡ A754
♢ J3
♣ QJ832

♠ J432
♡ J
♢ KQ1097
♣ 965

♠ A10985
♡ K108
♢ 65
♣ 1074

♠ Q7
♡ Q9632
♢ A842
♣ AK

West	North	East	South
–	–	–	1♡
Pass	4♡	All Pass	

Your partner, West, leads the king of diamonds against South's four hearts. Declarer wins with the ace in hand and plays a heart to dummy's ace (your partner playing the jack) followed by another heart. Plan the defence.

This is quite a common type of problem and it is difficult to think about when you are fairly new to the game. The point is that you know exactly how to beat four hearts: you know you can go in with the king of hearts, play a diamond to your partner's queen and he can play another diamond which you will ruff with your ten of hearts (surely partner would have bid if he had seven diamonds, thus giving declarer only a doubleton too). Then you will cash your ace of clubs as the setting trick.

When you know exactly what to do in defence it is time to stop and make sure that partner will know what to do as well. What can go wrong if you simply win the king of hearts and play a diamond? Well, partner might not be able to tell whether you started with two or four diamonds. He may think that you are trying to put him in in order for him to play a spade, for example. You need to wake him up.

Cash the ace of spades before playing back a diamond. Now he will know that you cannot want him to play a black suit – declarer must have something for his opening bid after all. The only line of defence open to him will be to give you a diamond ruff.

Problem 27

North/South Game. Dealer East.

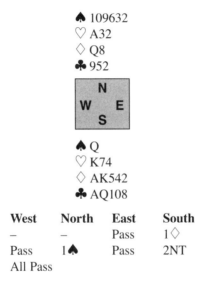

♠ 109632
♡ A32
◇ Q8
♣ 952

♠ Q
♡ K74
◇ AK542
♣ AQ108

West	North	East	South
–	–	Pass	1◇
Pass	1♠	Pass	2NT
All Pass			

South has an awkward choice of rebid after his partner's one spade response. Quite reasonably, he decided to describe his hand as a balanced 17–19 rather than rebid his clubs and get involved in what could be a complicated auction.

West leads the queen of hearts. Over to you.

Solution 27

North/South Game. Dealer East.

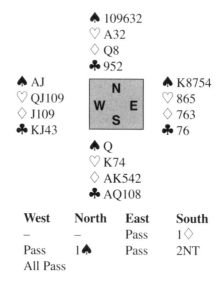

♠ 109632
♡ A32
◇ Q8
♣ 952

♠ AJ
♡ QJ109
◇ J109
♣ KJ43

♠ K8754
♡ 865
◇ 763
♣ 76

♠ Q
♡ K74
◇ AK542
♣ AQ108

West	North	East	South
–	–	Pass	1◇
Pass	1♠	Pass	2NT
All Pass			

West leads the queen of hearts against two no-trumps. Over to you.

You have six tricks on top: two hearts, three diamonds and a club. There are two main possibilities for extra tricks: play for diamonds to break 3-3 or play for East to have one of the club honours. Which chance should you take?

You do not have to make your decision immediately. Duck the opening lead (it cannot cost and is good general technique) and win the heart continuation with dummy's ace. Play a low club to your ten. Suppose this loses to West's jack and he continues with a third heart. You win in hand and now have to decide whether to play for diamonds 3-3 or the king of clubs with East.

The odds of a suit breaking 3-3 are 35.5%; while the odds of East having the king of clubs is 50%. You can narrow the gap between the percentage chances of these two lines by cashing the ace of clubs before playing for diamonds 3-3 (thus succeeding when anyone began with Kx of clubs) but the odds still favour a second club finesse.

So, cross to dummy's queen of diamonds and play the nine of clubs, underplaying with your eight if East plays small. If the nine of clubs holds, take another club finesse for your contract.

Oh dear, this time West had both club honours and diamonds broke 3-3. You went down in a cold contract. Never mind, bridge is a game of percentages. Correct plays do not win all of the time and at least you have the satisfaction of knowing you played well even if it was not successful this time.

Problem 28

Love All. Dealer South.

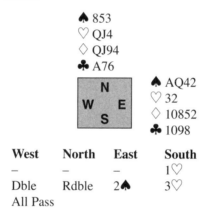

♠ 853
♡ QJ4
◇ QJ94
♣ A76

♠ AQ42
♡ 32
◇ 10852
♣ 1098

West	North	East	South
–	–	–	1♡
Dble	Rdble	2♠	3♡
All Pass			

After a spirited auction your opponents come to rest in three hearts. Once North has redoubled, a jump by your hand does not promise the earth – a decent suit to help with the lead will do. Your partner leads the jack of spades. Plan the defence.

Solution 28

Love All. Dealer South.

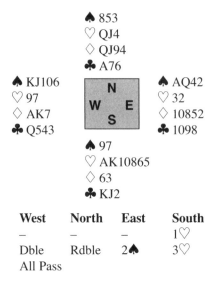

♠ 853
♡ QJ4
◇ QJ94
♣ A76

♠ KJ106
♡ 97
◇ AK7
♣ Q543

♠ AQ42
♡ 32
◇ 10852
♣ 1098

♠ 97
♡ AK10865
◇ 63
♣ KJ2

West	North	East	South
–	–	–	1♡
Dble	Rdble	2♠	3♡
All Pass			

After a spirited auction your opponents come to rest in three hearts. Your partner leads the jack of spades. Plan the defence.

It is hard to imagine that South has a heart loser on this bidding and he surely has at least a six-card suit. It seems clear that if left to his own devices declarer will make two diamond tricks to go with his six hearts and the ace of clubs. So the time has come to get active.

The only suit in which you can *develop* any tricks is clubs. So it looks clear to win the spade and switch to a club. The problem is that partner probably does not have the king and queen of clubs or he might have led one of them. If he has the king alone, one lead from you is sufficient; if he has the king and jack, you need to lead the suit *twice* through declarer. Alternatively, if he has the queen as his only honour, you need to lead the suit *twice* through declarer; but, if he has the queen and jack, one lead from you is sufficient.

So, on two of the hoped-for layouts you need to lead the suit twice. In most of the hoped-for layouts only three tricks are anticipated from the minors. If that is the case, then you need to hope that you have two spade tricks. You also have to pay some attention to making sure partner does not go wrong.

If you win the ace of spades and switch to the ten of clubs, when he has the actual hand above he may think you have the king of clubs and not the queen of spades. The way to make life easy for him is to play the *queen* of spades at trick one. There is no danger of this losing to declarer's singleton king as there is no way partner would make a take-out double with a five-card spade suit (on a minimum hand). When the queen of spades holds, switch to the ten of clubs. Declarer will win his king, draw two rounds of trumps and play a diamond. Your partner will win the diamond and play a second spade. You win your ace and play another club, setting up partner's queen for him to cash when he gets in with the ace of diamonds.

Problem 29

East/West Game. Dealer East.

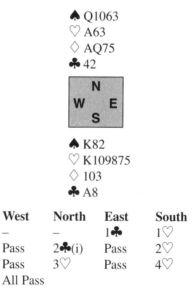

♠ Q1063
♡ A63
◇ AQ75
♣ 42

♠ K82
♡ K109875
◇ 103
♣ A8

West	North	East	South
–	–	1♣	1♡
Pass	2♣(i)	Pass	2♡
Pass	3♡	Pass	4♡
All Pass			

(i) unassuming cue-bid

Against your four hearts, West leads the seven of clubs, East playing the ten. How are you going to make your ambitious game?

Solution 29

East/West Game. Dealer East.

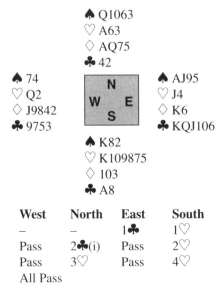

```
                    ♠ Q1063
                    ♡ A63
                    ◇ AQ75
                    ♣ 42
      ♠ 74              N            ♠ AJ95
      ♡ Q2                           ♡ J4
      ◇ J9842      W       E         ◇ K6
      ♣ 9753           S             ♣ KQJ106
                    ♠ K82
                    ♡ K109875
                    ◇ 103
                    ♣ A8
```

West	North	East	South
–	–	1♣	1♡
Pass	2♣(i)	Pass	2♡
Pass	3♡	Pass	4♡
All Pass			

(i) unassuming cue-bid

Against your four hearts, West leads the seven of clubs, East playing the ten. How are you going to make your ambitious game?

It looks as if you have a trick to lose in each side suit, so you must hope to bring in trumps for no loser. If East has the jack of spades you are going to need an endplay as well.

The first thing to do is to duck the ten of clubs. You do not want to risk West gaining the lead at a crucial stage later. Win the club continuation and cash the ace and king of trumps, being ready to finesse if an honour drops from West on the first round. They break and one potential loser has disappeared. Now play the king of spades. If East wins he is endplayed immediately, so he does best to duck. You then continue with a spade to the ten. If the finesse is successful, well and good, but if it isn't and East wins with his jack he is endplayed; he either has to give dummy a spade or a diamond trick, or else give you a ruff and discard.

Problem 30

This hand is presented as a two-part problem. First what would you lead as West:

Game All. Dealer South.

♠ 753
♡ 543
◇ K84
♣ K832

West	North	East	South
–	–	–	2♣(i)
Pass	2◇	Pass	2♡
Pass	2NT(ii)	Pass	4♣
Pass	5♣	Pass	6♣
All Pass			

(i) Acol   (ii) second negative

-o-o-o-o-o-

When trying to make an attacking lead against a slam it is usually best to go for the suit in which you have the most significant honour, because that is where you will need the least from partner. With two equal honours choose the shorter suit because any trick developed is more likely to stand up. Here the best lead is a diamond, after which you see the following dummy:

♠ 10964
♡ 8
◇ QJ1075
♣ 764

♠ 753
♡ 543
◇ K84
♣ K832

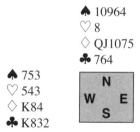

North might have shown his diamonds on the second round but the 'save space' two no-trumps allowed his partner to describe his hand more accurately in one bid. Declarer plays the queen of diamonds from the dummy and ruffs away partner's ace. He then cashes the ace of hearts and ruffs a heart, and plays a club to partner's ten and his queen. Over to you?

Solution 30

Game All. Dealer South.

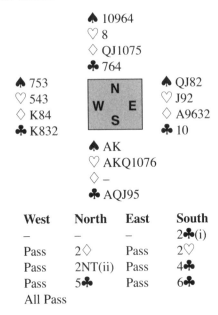

♠ 10964
♡ 8
◇ QJ1075
♣ 764

♠ 753
♡ 543
◇ K84
♣ K832

♠ QJ82
♡ J92
◇ A9632
♣ 10

♠ AK
♡ AKQ1076
◇ –
♣ AQJ95

West	North	East	South
–	–	–	2♣(i)
Pass	2◇	Pass	2♡
Pass	2NT(ii)	Pass	4♣
Pass	5♣	Pass	6♣
All Pass			

(i) Acol   (ii) second negative

You lead a diamond against South's slam. The queen is played from dummy and declarer ruffs away partner's ace. He then cashes the ace of hearts and ruffs a heart and plays a club to partner's ten and his queen. Over to you?

The hand is more or less an open book. You know that declarer started with five clubs, and your well-reasoned opening lead reduced that number to four. If you win the king of clubs and play the king of diamonds, you will have one more trump than declarer and must defeat the contract.

Note that had your trump spots been slightly weaker (interchange your eight with dummy's seven, for example), an expert declarer would still have been able to succeed, provided he took your partner's ten of clubs at face value and played for trumps to be 4-1. He starts by playing off some hearts. As soon as you discard one spade, he cashes the ace and king of spades. Then he plays his penultimate heart. If you discard a diamond, so does he and then he makes the last three tricks on a cross-ruff. So you must ruff the heart. Declarer overruffs, cashes a winning diamond from the dummy to discard his remaining heart, and makes the last two tricks with the ace and jack of clubs.

If your trump spots had been weaker, a better defence is to duck the queen of clubs smoothly. This makes it more difficult but an expert declarer can still succeed if he reads the hand perfectly.

Problem 31

Love All. Dealer South.

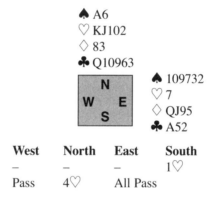

♠ A6
♡ KJ102
◇ 83
♣ Q10963

♠ 109732
♡ 7
◇ QJ95
♣ A52

West	North	East	South
–	–	–	1♡
Pass	4♡	All Pass	

Against South's four hearts, West leads the four of clubs. Can you see you best chance of four defensive tricks?

Solution 31

Love All. Dealer South.

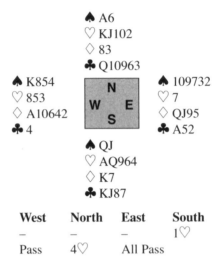

♠ A6
♡ KJ102
◇ 83
♣ Q10963

♠ K854
♡ 853
◇ A10642
♣ 4

♠ 109732
♡ 7
◇ QJ95
♣ A52

♠ QJ
♡ AQ964
◇ K7
♣ KJ87

West	North	East	South
–	–	–	1♡
Pass	4♡	All Pass	

Against South's four hearts, West leads the four of clubs. Can you see your best chance of four defensive tricks?

It looks as though partner's four of clubs is a singleton, so you could win the ace and give him a ruff. Can you think of anything better?

In order to beat the contract you need to take four tricks, not just two. If you assume that declarer has five hearts and that partner would have overcalled with either a five-card spade suit or a six-card diamond suit, then partner must be 4-3-5-1 in distribution. If so, there are two possibilities for him if you are to beat four hearts: maybe he has the ace of diamonds, or maybe he has the king of diamonds and ace of hearts (the king of *spades* and ace of hearts is no good, for you will not be able both to lead a spade through *and* give him a club ruff.

If he has the ace of hearts and king of diamonds, it works OK for you to give him a club ruff with your two. He can then switch to a diamond setting up a trick for him to cash when in with the ace of hearts. However, if he just has the ace of diamonds you must switch to the queen of diamonds now. Whether or not declarer covers, you will be able to deliver the club ruff either on the next round or the one after.

Which play should you go for? Definitely the latter, because it also works when declarer has the ace of diamonds and the ace of hearts. If declarer ducks, you give a club ruff; if he wins the ace of diamonds and plays a trump, partner can underlead his king of diamonds to get his club ruff.

Problem 32

Love All. Dealer North.

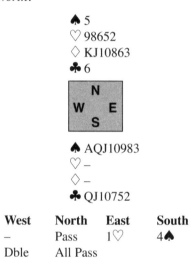

♠ 5
♡ 98652
♢ KJ10863
♣ 6

♠ AQJ10983
♡ –
♢ –
♣ QJ10752

West	North	East	South
–	Pass	1♡	4♠
Dble	All Pass		

Facing a passed partner, you decide on the simple jump to game with your freakish distribution and are rewarded when West's penalty double is left in.

West leads the ten of hearts and North reluctantly tables his dummy. Plan the play.

Solution 32

Love All. Dealer North.

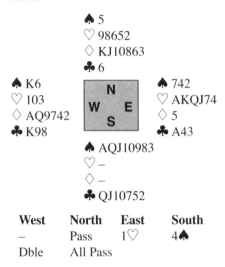

♠ 5
♡ 98652
◇ KJ10863
♣ 6

♠ K6
♡ 103
◇ AQ9742
♣ K98

♠ 742
♡ AKQJ74
◇ 5
♣ A43

♠ AQJ10983
♡ –
◇ –
♣ QJ10752

West	North	East	South
–	Pass	1♡	4♠
Dble	All Pass		

West leads the ten of hearts and North reluctantly tables his dummy. Plan the play.

Suppose you ruff the heart lead and play the jack of clubs from hand. West wins with the king and continues with the three of hearts which again you ruff. What now?

Careless play here could result in disaster. It looks tempting to ruff a club in the dummy but look what happens. You ruff a club in dummy and come back to hand with, say, a diamond ruff. Now you play the ace and jack of spades but West wins and forces you again (with the ace of diamonds). Now you have just one trump left. If you use it to draw the last trump, the defenders will have a herd of red-suit winners to cash when they are in with the ace of clubs.

You should forgo the club ruff in dummy. Simply ruff the second heart and play the ace and jack of spades. West can win and force you again but you ruff and now have two trumps left. Draw the remaining trump and give up a club. When the suit breaks 3-3 you have made your doubled game.

In the other room, where the double showed cards rather than penalty, East removed to five hearts which went one off.

Problem 33

North/South Game. Dealer West.

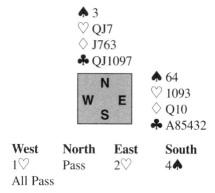

♠ 3
♡ QJ7
◇ J763
♣ QJ1097

♠ 64
♡ 1093
◇ Q10
♣ A85432

West	North	East	South
1♡	Pass	2♡	4♠
All Pass			

West cashes the king of hearts and switches to the king of clubs. Plan the defence.

Solution 33

North/South Game. Dealer West.

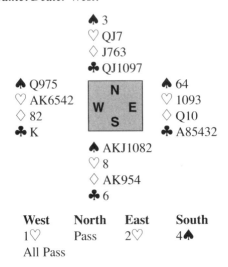

```
              ♠ 3
              ♡ QJ7
              ◇ J763
              ♣ QJ1097
♠ Q975          N          ♠ 64
♡ AK6542    W       E      ♡ 1093
◇ 82            S          ◇ Q10
♣ K                        ♣ A85432
              ♠ AKJ1082
              ♡ 8
              ◇ AK954
              ♣ 6
```

West	North	East	South
1♡	Pass	2♡	4♠
All Pass			

West cashes the king of hearts and switches to the king of clubs. Plan the defence.

Presumably the defence has only one heart trick or West would have cashed a second heart before playing a club. If we don't have a club trick it is hard to see where our four defensive tricks are coming from. Overtake the club (a Polish International master failed to do so in the European Pairs and the contract made) and now what?

Although declarer's clubs are now established there is no way for him to reach them unless the jack of diamonds is an entry. If declarer plays diamonds then West will make whatever tricks he has in that suit; however, if West doesn't have any diamond tricks then the only hope for two more tricks is to play another club and hope that partner's spades can be promoted into two trump tricks. You return a club but the defence is not over yet. Success will come only if partner doesn't carelessly overruff declarer's jack or ten. If he does, then declarer's three remaining honours will draw all West's trumps. If he refuses to overruff then, after declarer cashes the ace and king of spades, West will have the queen-nine as a tenace over declarer's remaining honour.

There are other positions where refusing to overruff generates a second trick – for example K109 over the AQJ when declarer ruffs with a minor honour. In any case, good technique says that you shouldn't overruff even if a second trick isn't possible; shortening declarer's trump length relative to yours may prove troublesome later.

Problem 34

North/South Game. Dealer South.

♠ 75
♡ 53
♢ AQJ8764
♣ J7

♠ A9
♡ AKJ8764
♢ 1093
♣ 6

West	North	East	South
–	–	–	1♡
Pass	2♢	Pass	3♡
Pass	4♡	All Pass	

There are those who would respond one no-trump on the North hand but two diamonds is a better effort with such a good suit. Here it enabled you to upgrade your hand because of the partial diamond fit and the excellent four hearts was reached.

West leads the king of clubs and switches to the five of diamonds. Plan the play.

Solution 34

North/South Game. Dealer South.

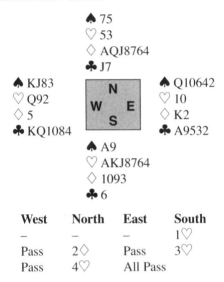

♠ 75
♡ 53
◇ AQJ8764
♣ J7

♠ KJ83
♡ Q92
◇ 5
♣ KQ1084

♠ Q10642
♡ 10
◇ K2
♣ A9532

♠ A9
♡ AKJ8764
◇ 1093
♣ 6

West	North	East	South
–	–	–	1♡
Pass	2◇	Pass	3♡
Pass	4♡	All Pass	

Against your four hearts West leads the king of clubs and switches to the five of diamonds. Plan the play.

It looks as though West has switched to a singleton diamond (though it could be 52 doubleton or even K52), so the first instinct is to rise with dummy's ace. At the table, this is what declarer did. He then cashed the ace and king of hearts but when the queen did not drop he had to go one down as East switched to a spade when in with the king of diamonds. West ruffed in on the diamonds and cashed a spade before declarer could discard his spade loser.

The diamond ruff was not something declarer should have been afraid of. Had he finessed at trick two and East given his partner a diamond ruff, then four hearts would have been cold with the queen of hearts now dropping under the ace-king. The diamonds would have been good for as many discards as declarer needed. Declarer should have finessed the diamond and left it up to East to find the winning defence of switching to a spade rather than giving his partner a diamond ruff.

You may think it wrong of West to switch to his singleton in dummy's suit, but had you, as declarer, had a doubleton diamond the switch would have killed the dummy and worked very well.

Problem 35

Love All. Dealer West.

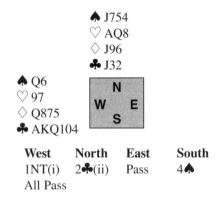

♠ J754
♡ AQ8
◇ J96
♣ J32

♠ Q6
♡ 97
◇ Q875
♣ AKQ104

West	North	East	South
1NT(i)	2♣(ii)	Pass	4♠
All Pass			

(i) 12–14   (ii) shows spades

You might not think a lot of the one no-trump opening I inflicted on you. You might think even less of North's contribution to the auction – this does not look to me like a hand with which anyone sane would want to come in over a 12–14 one no-trump, but this is bridge as it is played in some parts of the real world!

Anyway, you have a pretty stand-out lead of a top club on which you partner played the eight and declarer the seven. You persist with a second club which declarer ruffs. He then crosses to dummy's ace of hearts (partner playing the two) and plays a spade to his ten and your queen. What now?

Solution 35

Love All. Dealer West.

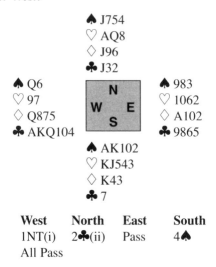

♠ J754
♡ AQ8
◇ J96
♣ J32

♠ Q6
♡ 97
◇ Q875
♣ AKQ104

♠ 983
♡ 1062
◇ A102
♣ 9865

♠ AK102
♡ KJ543
◇ K43
♣ 7

West	North	East	South
1NT(i)	2♣(ii)	Pass	4♠
All Pass			

(i) 12–14   (ii) shows spades

You lead a top club on which your partner played the eight and declarer the seven. You persist with a second club which declarer ruffs. He then crosses to dummy's ace of hearts (partner playing the two) and plays a spade to his ten and your queen. What now?

When dummy comes down and you think he is stark raving mad, it is very easy to relax and expect to beat declarer's contract whatever you do. It is surprising how often declarer has compensating values and the final contract is actually reasonable. Here at the table, I (Sally) carelessly continued with a third club. Declarer ruffed in hand, cashed the ace of spades, crossed to dummy's queen of hearts, drew the last trump and ran his hearts. Two of dummy's diamond losers went on the hearts.

Declarer's play at trick three suggested he had five good hearts – partner's two showed an odd number and if he had five hearts and a smattering of values he would probably have bid two hearts over two clubs. It also looked as if declarer would have one top diamond but not both – partner would probably have doubled four spades with an ace and a king, knowing that the opposition had at most a combined 19-count and only an eight-card fit.

What I should have done when in with the queen of spade was attack declarer's communications by playing a second heart. If declarer wins in dummy and plays a diamond he will lose a heart ruff. If he wins in hand, plays one round of trumps and then a third round of hearts to dummy before playing a diamond, East can rise with the ace of diamonds and play a third round of clubs forcing declarer to ruff in hand with his remaining top spade. Now declarer can't get to dummy to draw the last trump.

It is surprising how often playing declarer's best suit can work to advantage.

Problem 36

Game All. Dealer West.

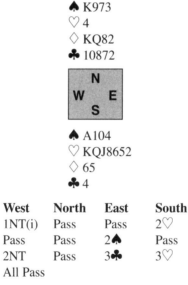

♠ K973
♡ 4
◇ KQ82
♣ 10872

♠ A104
♡ KQJ8652
◇ 65
♣ 4

West	North	East	South
1NT(i)	Pass	Pass	2♡
Pass	Pass	2♠	Pass
2NT	Pass	3♣	3♡
All Pass			

(i) 12–14

West leads the eight of spades against your three hearts. Plan the play.

Solution 36

Game All. Dealer West.

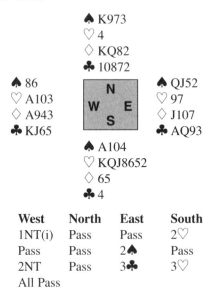

♠ K973
♡ 4
◇ KQ82
♣ 10872

♠ 86
♡ A103
◇ A943
♣ KJ65

♠ QJ52
♡ 97
◇ J107
♣ AQ93

♠ A104
♡ KQJ8652
◇ 65
♣ 4

West	North	East	South
1NT(i)	Pass	Pass	2♡
Pass	Pass	2♠	Pass
2NT	Pass	3♣	3♡
All Pass			

(i) 12–14

West leads the eight of spades against your three hearts. Plan the play.

For a start, the bidding is interesting. It is a good policy when playing a weak no-trump always to remove to two of a major with a five-card suit, therefore when East bids two spades on the second round he must have only a four-card suit. West's two no-trumps shows a doubleton spade only and suggests that East should try something else. When East bids three clubs the fit is found and South decides his seven-card suit merits further competition.

The play is straightforward provided declarer counts his tricks and bothers to make a plan. Suppose he carelessly lets the opening lead come round to his hand and plays the king of hearts. West will win and play a second spade. Declarer will have to win with the king and cannot get off the dummy. If he plays the king of diamonds, West will win, play a club to East's ace and now the queen of spades followed by a fourth round of the suit will promote a trick for West's ten of hearts.

All declarer has to do is win the opening lead in the *dummy* and play a trump. He wins the spade return in hand, draws trumps and establishes a diamond for his ninth trick.

Problem 37

East/West Game. Dealer South.

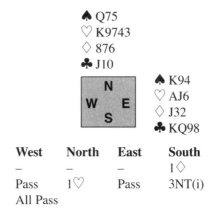

♠ Q75
♡ K9743
♢ 876
♣ J10

♠ K94
♡ AJ6
♢ J32
♣ KQ98

West	North	East	South
–	–	–	1♢
Pass	1♡	Pass	3NT(i)
All Pass			

(i) based on a long good diamond suit

Against South's three no-trumps, your partner leads the six of clubs. Plan the defence.

Solution 37

East/West Game. Dealer South.

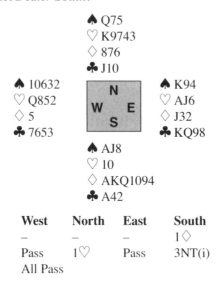

♠ Q75
♡ K9743
◇ 876
♣ J10

♠ 10632
♡ Q852
◇ 5
♣ 7653

♠ K94
♡ AJ6
◇ J32
♣ KQ98

♠ AJ8
♡ 10
◇ AKQ1094
♣ A42

West	North	East	South
–	–	–	1◇
Pass	1♡	Pass	3NT(i)
All Pass			

(i) based on a long good diamond suit

Against South's three no-trumps, your partner leads the six of clubs. Plan the defence.

At the table East covered dummy's jack with the queen and, when declarer ducked, continued with the king and nine of clubs. Declarer won the third round and ran all his diamonds. East could discard a spade and a heart, but the last diamond sunk him completely. He in fact pitched his long club but declarer now ducked a heart to East who, after cashing his ace, was forced to lead a spade round to dummy's queen.

East could have foreseen this ending. His only chance was to hope that declarer had a singleton heart (fairly likely on the bidding). When declarer ducks the second club, East should cash the ace of hearts before exiting with a club. Now on the run of the diamonds East can pitch two hearts and a spade. Declarer then has to play a spade and there are five defensive tricks.

Of course, declarer could have foiled this plan by winning the *second* club. Now East cannot escape the endplay. It would not help him to cash the ace of hearts at trick two because then he would be thrown in with a club instead.

On a slightly different note, the actual East made it very easy for declarer to read the end position. When you are in this type of position and know you are going to be squeezed, it is best to pretend your distribution is different from what it actually is and discard accordingly. Here East should set about pretending that he started with four spades and two hearts. On the run of the diamonds he should have discarded the nine followed by the four of spades and then a heart. There is then a fair chance declarer will duck a heart to him, hoping to endplay him into leading away from his supposed doubleton king of spades.

When you have all the defensive high cards it is easy to falsecard because it does not matter if partner is misled.

Problem 38

Love All. Dealer West.

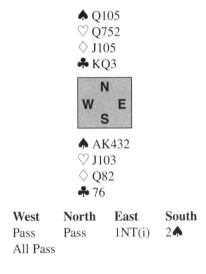

```
              ♠ Q105
              ♡ Q752
              ◇ J105
              ♣ KQ3
                 N
              W     E
                 S
              ♠ AK432
              ♡ J103
              ◇ Q82
              ♣ 76
```

West	North	East	South
Pass	Pass	1NT(i)	2♠
All Pass			

(i) 12–14

West leads a low club against your two spades – not a bid to be recommended except to the most intrepid! Dummy's king loses to the ace and East returns a second club. Plan the play.

Solution 38

Love All. Dealer West.

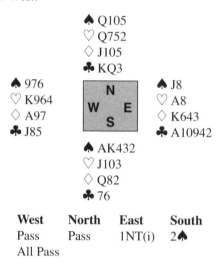

♠ Q105
♡ Q752
◇ J105
♣ KQ3

♠ 976
♡ K964
◇ A97
♣ J85

♠ J8
♡ A8
◇ K643
♣ A10942

♠ AK432
♡ J103
◇ Q82
♣ 76

West	North	East	South
Pass	Pass	1NT(i)	2♠
All Pass			

(i) 12–14

West leads a low club against your two spades. Dummy's king loses to the ace and East returns a second club. Plan the play.

It looks as if you have only five losers, so maybe you should just draw trumps and set about your red suits. The problem with this plan is that you will run out of trumps. Suppose you win the queen of clubs and draw trumps. That will leave you with two trumps left in hand. Say you play a diamond. A defender wins and plays another club which you ruff. You play another diamond. A defender wins and plays another club removing your last trump. Now when a defender wins a heart he will have a club to cash (if clubs were 5-3 in the beginning). If clubs were 4-4 to start with, then when the defender wins the first heart trick he will play a diamond, knocking out your last stopper in the suit; then there will be a long diamond for the defenders to cash when in with the second heart honour. Maybe you should have started by playing on hearts but there could also be a third loser in that suit unless it breaks 3-3.

On the other hand, if you don't draw trumps you may find you lose a red-suit ruff, possibly in diamonds but more likely in hearts.

The (far from guaranteed) best solution is to draw just two rounds of trumps (with the ace and queen). This reduces the danger of losing a ruff but the third trump in dummy protects you from the force. After two rounds of trumps you play, say, a diamond. This loses and the defence persist with clubs. You ruff and play a second diamond. If the defenders play a fourth club you can take the ruff in the dummy. The best West can do is play a third round of trumps. You win in hand and play a heart, East can win and play a fourth club but he has no entry to get in to cash his established fifth card in the suit.

By leaving the ten of spades in the dummy you protect yourself from the force.

Problem 39

East/West Game. Pairs. Dealer West.

You, South, hold:

♠ KQ8
♡ QJ10
♢ 97
♣ QJ1072

What do you bid after the following sequence:

West	North	East	South
1NT(i)	Pass	2◇	Pass
2♡	Pass	Pass	?

(i) 12–14

Solution 39

East/West Game. Pairs. Dealer West.

You, South, hold:

♠ KQ8
♥ QJ10
♦ 97
♣ QJ1072

What do you bid after the following sequence:

West	North	East	South
1NT(i)	Pass	2♦	Pass
2♥	Pass	Pass	?

(i) 12–14

It looks very tempting to protect with three clubs at Pairs at favourable vulnerability. Indeed, if you do you find a pretty good dummy and make three or four clubs without too much difficulty. This was the full deal:

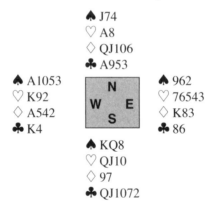

♠ J74
♥ A8
♦ QJ106
♣ A953

♠ A1053
♥ K92
♦ A542
♣ K4

♠ 962
♥ 76543
♦ K83
♣ 86

♠ KQ8
♥ QJ10
♦ 97
♣ QJ1072

So, a good hand for aggressive balancing? No, not really. If you look at the East/West cards you will see that you can hardly fail to take seven tricks against two hearts. It is not easy to see exactly how the play and defence will go but the cards do not lie well for declarer.

It is galling to score your pushy +130 and find you get a poor score because the score sheet is littered with –200s by East/West. Is there something to be learned from this result?

It is important to realise that favourable vulnerability is not the best time to consider a pushy partscore action. Love All is much better. Had this deal occurred at Love All you would have had a top because your +130 would have compared with –100s by the East/Wests. A huge difference in result for the same action.

The worst vulnerability for these sort of bids is Game All. At least at the actual vulnerability, if you had bought a very poor dummy and lost 100 you might have found that some East/Wests were making +110. At Game All you would have lost a 'kiss-of-death' 200.

Problem 40

Game All. Dealer North.

♠ 73
♡ AK6
◇ AK10
♣ A10853

♠ J1064
♡ QJ103
◇ J4
♣ Q94

West	North	East	South
–	1♣	Pass	1♡
Pass	2◇	Pass	3♣
Pass	3♡	Pass	3NT
All Pass			

Plan the play in three no-trumps on the three of diamonds lead.

Solution 40

Game All. Dealer North.

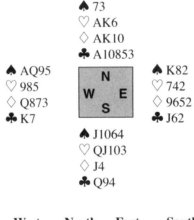

♠ 73
♡ AK6
◇ AK10
♣ A10853

♠ AQ95
♡ 985
◇ Q873
♣ K7

♠ K82
♡ 742
◇ 9652
♣ J62

♠ J1064
♡ QJ103
◇ J4
♣ Q94

West	North	East	South
–	1♣	Pass	1♡
Pass	2◇	Pass	3♣
Pass	3♡	Pass	3NT
All Pass			

Plan the play in three no-trumps on the three of diamonds lead.

It is likely that West has the queen of diamonds, so one possibility would be to run the opening lead round to your jack and try the queen of clubs from your hand. This is the best line of play in the club suit. Can you see a problem with this line?

The problem is that if East is allowed to win a club trick the defence may be in a position to take four spade tricks. However, the defenders can never take four spade tricks if the first lead in the suit comes from West.

So, there is no need to take any gratuitous risks in diamonds. Win the diamond lead with the ace and play a club to the nine at trick two. If the nine loses to the jack, you will have to run the queen later, hoping that West has the king as well as the jack.

PART THREE

Problem 41

East/West Game. Dealer South

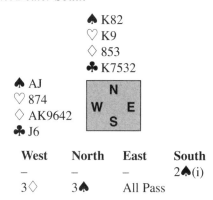

♠ K82
♡ K9
◇ 853
♣ K7532

♠ AJ
♡ 874
◇ AK9642
♣ J6

N
W E
S

West	North	East	South
–	–	–	2♠(i)
3◇	3♠	All Pass	

(i) weak

You lead the ace and king of diamonds as partner plays the ten and seven and declarer the queen and jack. Plan the defence.

Solution 41

East/West Game. Dealer South

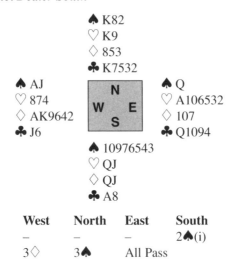

```
                      ♠ K82
                      ♡ K9
                      ◇ 853
                      ♣ K7532
   ♠ AJ                  N              ♠ Q
   ♡ 874        W              E        ♡ A106532
   ◇ AK9642                            ◇ 107
   ♣ J6                   S            ♣ Q1094
                      ♠ 10976543
                      ♡ QJ
                      ◇ QJ
                      ♣ A8
```

West	North	East	South
–	–	–	2♠(i)
3◇	3♠	All Pass	

(i) weak

You lead the ace and king of diamonds as partner plays the ten and seven and declarer the queen and jack. Plan the defence.

You have difficult choices, but with only three tricks in your hand you need partner to contribute at least two more. You could play a heart hoping that partner had the ace and queen with declarer holding at least a doubleton. You could play a club playing partner for the same holding in that suit and now you may be able to make the jack of spades on the third round. You could play a club and have partner play low with the ace, looking for a club ruff as your fifth trick. Alternatively, you could play another diamond hoping that partner could ruff with the queen of spades. Because you have the ace of trumps you have time to try two chances.

The best defence is to play a third diamond now, hoping partner has the queen of spades. If he doesn't, he may be able to signal to tell you which suit to try when you gain the lead with your ace of spades.

This time all is well as partner has the queen of spades.

Problem 42

East/West Game. Dealer East.

♠ AJ52
♡ QJ109
◇ Q74
♣ 64

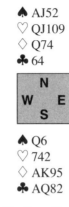

♠ Q6
♡ 742
◇ AK95
♣ AQ82

West	North	East	South
–	–	Pass	1◇
Pass	1♡	Pass	1NT
Pass	3NT	All Pass	

West leads the three of clubs against your three no-trumps. East plays the nine and you win with the queen. Plan the play.

-o-o-o-o-o-

You do not have nine tricks without developing at least one in hearts. The best you can hope for outside the heart suit are two spades, four diamonds and two clubs. So at trick two you play a heart to the queen and East's ace. East continues with the jack of clubs. What now?

Solution 42

East/West Game. Dealer East.

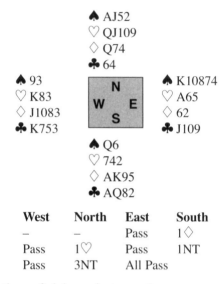

♠ AJ52
♡ QJ109
♢ Q74
♣ 64

♠ 93
♡ K83
♢ J1083
♣ K753

♠ K10874
♡ A65
♢ 62
♣ J109

♠ Q6
♡ 742
♢ AK95
♣ AQ82

West	North	East	South
–	–	Pass	1♢
Pass	1♡	Pass	1NT
Pass	3NT	All Pass	

West leads the three of clubs against your three no-trumps. East plays the nine and you win with the queen. At trick two you play a heart to the queen and East's ace. East continues with the jack of clubs. What now?

East has very kindly told you exactly the layout of the club suit. The only holding consistent with his play is J109. If you duck this club, as is perhaps the reflex action, he will play another, knocking out your ace. Now when West gets in with his presumed king of hearts he will be able to cash a club. Then you will need either a 3-3 diamond break or the spade finesse for your contract.

Much better is to win the jack of clubs with the ace. Now when you play a heart West can win his king and play a club to his partner's ten, but the suit is blocked. Whatever East returns at this stage you can win and take a spade finesse, establishing a certain nine tricks whether it wins or loses. (It would be an error to test diamonds first because in so doing you might set up a diamond winner for East to cash when he is in with his king of spades.)

Problem 43

Game All. Dealer South.

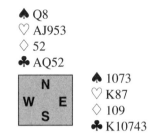

                    ♠ Q8
                    ♡ AJ953
                    ◇ 52
                    ♣ AQ52
                                        ♠ 1073
                                        ♡ K87
                                        ◇ 109
                                        ♣ K10743

West	North	East	South
–	–	–	2◇(i)
Pass	2♡	Pass	3◇
Pass	4♣	Pass	4◇
Pass	4NT	Pass	5♡(ii)
Pass	5NT	Pass	6◇(iii)
	All Pass		

(i) Acol   (ii) 2 aces   (iii) 1 king

Against South's slam, your partner, West, leads the eight of clubs. Declarer plays low from the dummy and you …

Solution 43

Game All. Dealer South.

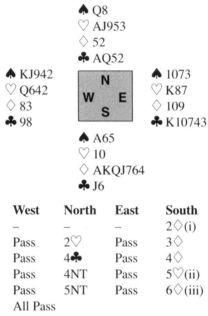

```
              ♠ Q8
              ♡ AJ953
              ◇ 52
              ♣ AQ52
  ♠ KJ942                      ♠ 1073
  ♡ Q642         N            ♡ K87
  ◇ 83       W       E        ◇ 109
  ♣ 98           S            ♣ K10743
              ♠ A65
              ♡ 10
              ◇ AKQJ764
              ♣ J6
```

West	North	East	South
–	–	–	2◇(i)
Pass	2♡	Pass	3◇
Pass	4♣	Pass	4◇
Pass	4NT	Pass	5♡(ii)
Pass	5NT	Pass	6◇(iii)
All Pass			

(i) Acol   (ii) 2 aces   (iii) 1 king

Against South's slam, your partner, West, leads the eight of clubs. Declarer plays low from the dummy and you ...

It looks as if your partner has led top of a doubleton. This does not seem the moment for an erudite duck, so you win your king of clubs and declarer plays the six.

Declarer has shown two aces and one king. If his king is in spades there is no problem in the defence for your partner will make his king of diamonds for the setting trick. So you must assume that declarer has the king of diamonds, and probably the queen as well. He seems to be pretty minimum for an Acol two-bid so it is reasonable to assume that he has seven diamonds. You can see he has twelve tricks: seven diamonds, one spade, one heart and three clubs (since he must have the jack).

The only hope is to sever his communications. You need to remove dummy's ace of hearts *now*. So, at trick two you must switch to a heart, but which heart? If you switch to a low heart and declarer has the singleton ten, that card will force partner's queen. Declarer will then be able to take a ruffing finesse of your king. No, the correct switch is to the *king* of hearts. Now whatever declarer does he has to lose another trick. (His best chance is that your partner had an initial *four*-card club holding along with the king of spades, in which case cashing his ace of spades and running his diamonds would squeeze him in the black suits. No luck this time.)

Problem 44

Game All. Dealer South.

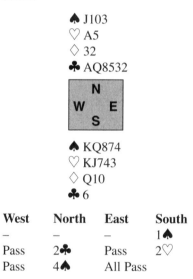

♠ J103
♥ A5
♦ 32
♣ AQ8532

♠ KQ874
♥ KJ743
♦ Q10
♣ 6

West	North	East	South
–	–	–	1♠
Pass	2♣	Pass	2♥
Pass	4♠	All Pass	

Against your four spades, West leads the eight of diamonds to the ace. East returns the five of diamonds to the king and West plays ace and another spade. Continue from here.

Solution 44

Game All. Dealer South.

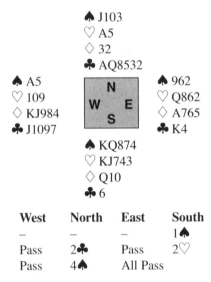

```
                    ♠ J103
                    ♡ A5
                    ◇ 32
                    ♣ AQ8532
        ♠ A5                      ♠ 962
        ♡ 109          N          ♡ Q862
        ◇ KJ984    W     E        ◇ A765
        ♣ J1097        S          ♣ K4
                    ♠ KQ874
                    ♡ KJ743
                    ◇ Q10
                    ♣ 6
```

West	North	East	South
–	–	–	1♠
Pass	2♣	Pass	2♡
Pass	4♠	All Pass	

Against your four spades, West leads the eight of diamonds to the ace. East returns the five of diamonds to the king and West plays ace and another spade. Continue from here.

It looks as if you have a choice of playing on hearts or clubs. You could play on hearts, by playing the ace and king and ruffing a heart, hoping for a 3-3 break or for the queen to drop doubleton (alternatively, you could take a heart finesse which would succeed whenever East held the queen, but this is not such a good chance. However, you could also cash the ace of clubs and ruff a club, then cross to the jack of spades and ruff another club. This would succeed whenever clubs were 3-3 or when the king dropped doubleton. Superficially these chances would seem to be equal. Which should you choose or can you see any way of combining your chances?

You cannot test hearts before you play on clubs because the ace of hearts is a key entry for the club play. But you can afford to ruff one club before playing on hearts. So the best line is to play on hearts, but to give yourself the extra chance of the king of clubs coming down doubleton.

So, win trick four with the jack of spades. Cash the ace of clubs and ruff a club high. Here the king comes down so you cross back to dummy with the ten of spades and ruff another club. Now dummy's club suit is established and you have made your game. If the king of clubs had not fallen, then you would have cashed the ace and king of hearts and ruffed a heart in the dummy, making whenever hearts were 3-3 or the queen dropped doubleton.

Problem 45

North/South Game. Dealer North.

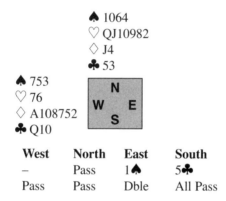

♠ 1064
♡ QJ10982
◇ J4
♣ 53

♠ 753
♡ 76
◇ A108752
♣ Q10

West	North	East	South
–	Pass	1♠	5♣
Pass	Pass	Dble	All Pass

Against South's five clubs doubled, you lead the five of spades. East wins with the nine and returns the four of clubs which declarer wins with the ace. Declarer continues with the six of diamonds to your eight, dummy's jack and partner's queen. Your partner plays the jack of spades which declarer ruffs and continues with the three of diamonds. Plan the defence.

Solution 45

North/South Game. Dealer North.

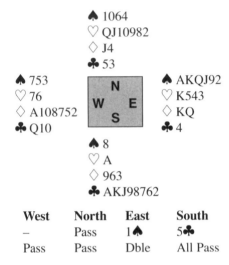

♠ 1064
♥ QJ10982
♦ J4
♣ 53

♠ 753 ♠ AKQJ92
♥ 76 ♥ K543
♦ A108752 ♦ KQ
♣ Q10 ♣ 4

♠ 8
♥ A
♦ 963
♣ AKJ98762

West	North	East	South
–	Pass	1♠	5♣
Pass	Pass	Dble	All Pass

Against South's five clubs doubled, you lead the five of spades. East wins with the nine and returns the four of clubs which declarer wins with the ace. Declarer continues with the six of diamonds to your eight, dummy's jack and partner's queen. Your partner plays the jack of spades which declarer ruffs and continues with the three of diamonds. Plan the defence.

At least you know for certain that five clubs is going down, but it also looks as if your side can make four spades, so you need to try to beat five clubs doubled by two tricks.

It looks certain that partner has a singleton club, giving declarer eight to go with the known singleton spade. Declarer has shown two small diamonds leaving him with two unknown red cards. If he has two hearts without both the ace or king he will always go two down as partner will eventually make a heart trick. Similarly if he has four diamonds he will always go two down, three down if we win this trick with the ten and play a second trump. But what about one heart and three diamonds? Now if he gets one ruff in dummy and his heart honour is the ace he will make ten tricks. We need to win this trick and play a trump to cater for all possible holdings but how do we win this trick? When South has three diamonds partner has a doubleton. If he has queen doubleton diamond we need to play the ten and if he has king-queen doubleton we need to play the ace, otherwise East would perforce have to overtake and we know that he doesn't have a trump to play. Which is it to be? Listen to the bidding. East doubled the final contract. He has excellent spades and no more than the king of hearts, so surely he needs the king and queen of diamonds. Rise with the ace and feel pleased when partner's king falls, but don't forget to play the second trump. Note that partner should have continued with the king of diamonds when he won the lead with the queen. There is no greater talent as a defender than not allowing partner the room to do the wrong thing!

This play, playing a higher card than necessary in order to 'swallow' partner's card which otherwise would get in the way and endplay him, is known as the Crocodile Coup.

Problem 46

East/West Game. Dealer South.

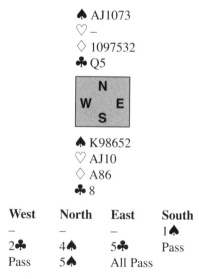

♠ AJ1073
♡ –
◇ 1097532
♣ Q5

♠ K98652
♡ AJ10
◇ A86
♣ 8

West	North	East	South
–	–	–	1♠
2♣	4♠	5♣	Pass
Pass	5♠	All Pass	

You could have beaten five clubs by a trick but your partner decided to press on to five spades. West starts with the ace of clubs and a club to his partner's king. Can you justify your partner's confidence in your dummy play?

Solution 46

East/West Game. Dealer South.

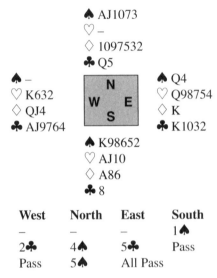

♠ AJ1073
♡ –
◇ 1097532
♣ Q5

♠ –
♡ K632
◇ QJ4
♣ AJ9764

♠ Q4
♡ Q98754
◇ K
♣ K1032

♠ K98652
♡ AJ10
◇ A86
♣ 8

West	North	East	South
–	–	–	1♠
2♣	4♠	5♣	Pass
Pass	5♠	All Pass	

You could have beaten five clubs by a trick but your partner, not unreasonably, decided to press on to five spades. West starts with the ace of clubs and a second club to his partner's king. Can you justify your partner's confidence in your declarer play?

Obviously everything will be fine if diamonds break 2-2 but can you see any chances if they are 3-1?

This is a neat variation of a standard elimination. Ruff the second club, and ruff a heart. Play the ace of spades and a spade to your king. Now cash the ace of hearts, pitching a diamond, and ruff your last heart. Now play a low diamond from both hands. If diamonds are 2-2, your ace will drop both remaining diamond honours on the next round; if one defender has a singleton honour you will also succeed because either he will be left on lead to give a ruff and discard, or his partner will overtake and either have to give a ruff and discard or else lead a diamond into the tenace that has been created by the overtaking play.

Note that this is fine in theory, but in practice is not 100%. Suppose East goes in with the king, West playing the jack, and continues with the four. Did he start with K4 doubleton or KQ4?

Problem 47

Game All. Dealer South.

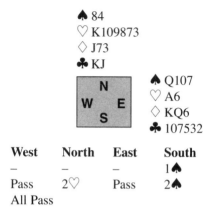

♠ 84
♡ K109873
♢ J73
♣ KJ

♠ Q107
♡ A6
♢ KQ6
♣ 107532

West	North	East	South
–	–	–	1♠
Pass	2♡	Pass	2♠
All Pass			

Against two spades your partner leads the six of clubs which declarer wins in the dummy with the king. At trick two he plays the eight of spades. Plan your defence.

Solution 47

Game All. Dealer South.

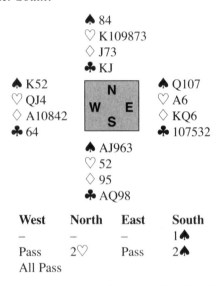

♠ 84
♡ K109873
◇ J73
♣ KJ

♠ K52
♡ QJ4
◇ A10842
♣ 64

♠ Q107
♡ A6
◇ KQ6
♣ 107532

♠ AJ963
♡ 52
◇ 95
♣ AQ98

West	North	East	South
–	–	–	1♠
Pass	2♡	Pass	2♠
All Pass			

Against two spades your partner leads the six of clubs which declarer wins in the dummy with the king. At trick two he plays the eight of spades. Plan your defence.

At one table East played a low spade and declarer ran the eight to West's king. West continued with a second club, again won in dummy. Declarer now played a spade to his jack, drew trumps and played a heart, making only eight tricks when the ace of hearts was wrong.

At the other table East was a little more awake and played the *queen* on the first round of spades. The play of a high honour from this holding (or K10x) is well known. The idea is to try to persuade declarer that your original holding was KQx so that he will play to his jack next time and so lose two trump tricks. While this might indeed be the case on this occasion, here the play of rising with the queen of trumps generates an extra trick for a different reason.

Declarer wins the queen of spades with the ace and crosses to dummy with a club to play a second spade. Even if he plays the nine, losing to West's king, West can put his partner in with a red suit to get a club ruff. One down.

Problem 48

East/West Game. Dealer South.

♠ 63
♡ 109852
◇ AQ1063
♣ 6

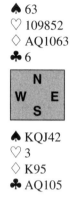

♠ KQJ42
♡ 3
◇ K95
♣ AQ105

West	North	East	South
–	–	–	1♠
Pass	1NT	Pass	2♣
Pass	2♠	Pass	3◇
Pass	4◇	Pass	4♠
All Pass			

A delicate sequence to a delicate game. West leads the four of hearts to East's queen and East switches to the four of clubs. Plan the play.

Solution 48

East/West Game. Dealer South.

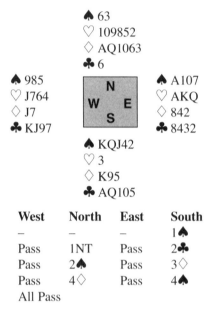

```
                 ♠ 63
                 ♡ 109852
                 ♢ AQ1063
                 ♣ 6
    ♠ 985                      ♠ A107
    ♡ J764         N           ♡ AKQ
    ♢ J7       W       E       ♢ 842
    ♣ KJ97         S           ♣ 8432
                 ♠ KQJ42
                 ♡ 3
                 ♢ K95
                 ♣ AQ105
```

West	North	East	South
–	–	–	1♠
Pass	1NT	Pass	2♣
Pass	2♠	Pass	3♢
Pass	4♢	Pass	4♠
All Pass			

A delicate sequence to a delicate game. West leads the four of hearts to East's queen and East switches to the four of clubs. Plan the play.

If spades are 4-2, which is unlikely since East didn't force you at trick two, you can never make the contract. Suppose a defender wins the second spade and forces you with a heart. You can't draw all the trumps without letting a defender in to cash a heart. If you simply play diamonds someone will ruff the third or fourth round and you will have to play clubs from your hand.

So, assume spades are 3-3. If you win the ace of clubs and try to ruff clubs in the dummy you may still lose a trump promotion or diamond ruff; alternatively, if you win the ace of clubs and play a spade, the defenders will surely duck until the second round and now you may go down if East has the ace of spades and West the king and jack of clubs (or if you guess wrongly).

The way to guarantee your contract whenever trumps are 3-3 is to finesse the club. West cannot profitably continue the suit and will probably continue with hearts. Now you ruff and play trumps. East can win his ace whenever he likes but can do you no harm. If he plays another heart, you ruff, draw trumps and run your diamonds; if he tries a second club, you win your ace and again draw trumps and run your diamonds.

Problem 49

North/South Game. Dealer East.

The bidding goes:

West	North	East	South
–	–	1$\diamondsuit$	Dble
1♠	Dble(i)	2$\diamondsuit$	2♠
Dble	Pass	Pass	3♣
?			

(i) shows four or more spades and a few values

What would you bid as West with the following hand?

♠ AKQJ9
♡ 109842
$\diamondsuit$ 103
♣ Q

Solution 49

North/South Game. Dealer East.

The bidding goes:

West	North	East	South
–	–	1♢	Dble
1♠	Dble(i)	2♢	2♠
Dble	Pass	Pass	3♣
?			

(i) shows four or more spades and a few values

What would you bid as West with the following hand?

♠ AKQJ9
♡ 109842
♢ 103
♣ Q

You might not fancy your trump holding, but this hand is perfect for a penalty double. The opponents' spades must be 4-4, so you can start by cashing four spade tricks. Surely that will allow partner to discard all his hearts, so then you can give him a heart ruff to beat the contract by one, even if partner has no defensive tricks at all – and he has opened the bidding.

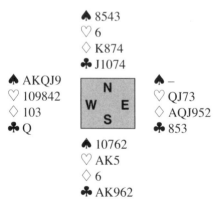

♠ 8543
♡ 6
♢ K874
♣ J1074

♠ AKQJ9
♡ 109842
♢ 103
♣ Q

♠ –
♡ QJ73
♢ AQJ952
♣ 853

♠ 10762
♡ AK5
♢ 6
♣ AK962

This hand comes from the 1989 Common Market Mixed Teams Championships when Bernard Goldenfield found the double to gain 2 IMPs for his team.

Problem 50

Love All. Dealer North.

♠ QJ1065
♡ AJ97
♢ A
♣ A42

West	North	East	South
–	1♠	Pass	2♢
Pass	2♠	Pass	2NT
All Pass			

This hand comes from the EBL Senior Pairs Championship. What would you lead against South's two no-trumps?

Solution 50

Love All. Dealer North.

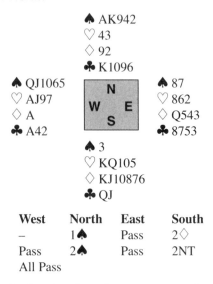

♠ AK942
♡ 43
◇ 92
♣ K1096

♠ QJ1065
♡ AJ97
◇ A
♣ A42

♠ 87
♡ 862
◇ Q543
♣ 8753

♠ 3
♡ KQ105
◇ KJ10876
♣ QJ

West	North	East	South
–	1♠	Pass	2◇
Pass	2♠	Pass	2NT
All Pass			

What would you lead against South's two no-trumps?

José Damiani, President of the World Bridge Federation, found the winning lead at the table. He led a low spade. Declarer rose with dummy's ace and ran the nine of diamonds to Damiani's ace. Damiani continued with another low spade. Declarer again played high from dummy, hoping to drop an honour from East. When this failed to materialise declarer had to go one down.

It can work well to lead low from a three-card honour sequence for another reason. Look at this deal:

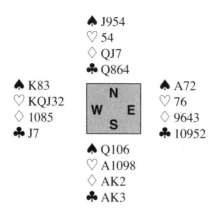

♠ J954
♡ 54
◇ QJ7
♣ Q864

♠ K83
♡ KQJ32
◇ 1085
♣ J7

♠ A72
♡ 76
◇ 9643
♣ 10952

♠ Q106
♡ A1098
◇ AK2
♣ AK3

Suppose the bidding has revealed that declarer has a four-card heart suit. If West leads a top heart, declarer will simply duck, thus killing any hope for the defence. On the other hand, if West leads a low heart, declarer needs to develop a spade for his ninth trick. When he plays a spade, East hops in with his ace and has a second heart to play so can clear the suit. Now when West gets the lead with his king of spades, he has three heart tricks to cash.

Problem 51

Love All. Dealer East. Pairs.

What would you bid as West with the following hand:

♠ AKQ104
♡ Q6
◇ A9542
♣ 8

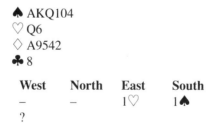

West	North	East	South
–	–	1♡	1♠
?			

Solution 51

Love All. Dealer East. Pairs.

What would you bid as West with the following hand:

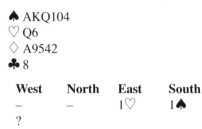

♠ AKQ104
♡ Q6
◇ A9542
♣ 8

West	North	East	South
–	–	1♡	1♠
?			

The answer is that if your system includes penalty doubles you should double, but if you are playing negative doubles, as is the norm these days, you should pass.

The negative double was introduced into expert play in 1957 by Alvin Roth and Tobias Stone. It was named Sputnik originally after the first satellite (launched by the USSR) at about that time. However, *The Official Encyclopedia of Bridge*, an invaluable reference book, tells us that the convention had been used by Lou Scharf of New York since as early as 1937.

The corollary that a pass of the simple overcall should be forcing on opener when he is short in the suit is not so widely understood. Without this agreement you lose all chance of taking a penalty from a simple overcall and when the opponents discover this they will bid against you as often as possible, at least non-vulnerable. Opener should double whenever he would have stood an old-fashioned penalty double. In other words, he makes a take-out double which, as with any take-out double, you may pass for penalties.

If we interchange the suits in the hand above to: ♠A9542 ♡Q6 ◇AKQ104 ♣8 there is still a case for starting with a pass of one spade since we 'know' that partner will bid again with his known spade shortage. However, with this hand, when partner re-opens with a double we might decide to look for better things and cue-bid two spades instead of passing. The only explanation for such bidding is that we have length in the opponent's suit. Such a cue-bid is best played as game forcing. If instead we held such as ♠J9543 ♡Q3 ◇AK753 ♣8 we simply jump to three diamonds on the second round, having first passed to show the spade length.

Opener is forced to re-open whenever he is short in the suit overcalled, since he could be facing a strong opening bid with length in the opponent's suit. However, he doesn't have to double. If he simply bids a suit, this shows a light distributional hand. Thus if he rebids Two Hearts on our first hand we are probably worth a splinter-bid in clubs. Alternatively, if opener has a strong distributional hand he can re-open with a jump bid which should be treated as non-forcing.

Problem 52

Love All. Dealer West.

♠ AJ1063
♡ A74
◇ QJ102
♣ 6

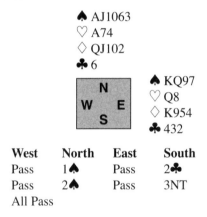

♠ KQ97
♡ Q8
◇ K954
♣ 432

West	North	East	South
Pass	1♠	Pass	2♣
Pass	2♠	Pass	3NT
All Pass			

Against South's three no-trumps, your partner, West, leads the six of diamonds. Declarer plays the queen from dummy, and you...

Solution 52

Love All. Dealer West.

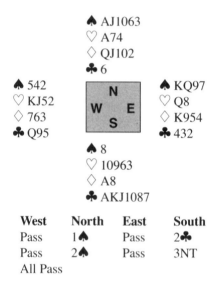

♠ AJ1063
♡ A74
◇ QJ102
♣ 6

♠ 542
♡ KJ52
◇ 763
♣ Q95

♠ KQ97
♡ Q8
◇ K954
♣ 432

♠ 8
♡ 10963
◇ A8
♣ AKJ1087

West	North	East	South
Pass	1♠	Pass	2♣
Pass	2♠	Pass	3NT
All Pass			

Against South's three no-trumps, your partner, West, leads the six of diamonds. Declarer plays the queen from dummy, and you...

It looks as if partner has led a diamond from either three small or a doubleton. It is not possible that he has led from four small because not only would that leave declarer with an unlikely singleton ace (unlikely both because of his bidding and the play of the queen from dummy), but it would also leave partner with 8763, a holding from which he would have led the seven, not the six.

Normal good technique would be not to cover the queen of diamonds, but is that the right thing to do here?

The reason for not covering the first of touching honours played by declarer is partly because declarer may have singleton ace and partly because it usually helps declarer unscramble his tricks. Here there is something else to take into consideration.

As you have the spade suit well sewn up, it is likely that declarer is going to need to set up some tricks in clubs in order to fulfil his contract. To do that he needs entries to his hand so it is in the defence's interests to force him to use them as soon as possible.

Here you should cover the queen of diamonds with the king. Once the ace of diamonds is removed, declarer has no chance of making his contract. Note that declarer has three, and only three, diamond tricks as of right, so covering the queen does not give him anything to which he is not entitled. If all he needed for his contract were three diamond tricks he could simply win the ace and play one back.

Problem 53

Love All. Dealer North.

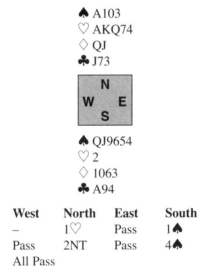

♠ A103
♡ AKQ74
◇ QJ
♣ J73

♠ QJ9654
♡ 2
◇ 1063
♣ A94

West	North	East	South
–	1♡	Pass	1♠
Pass	2NT	Pass	4♠
All Pass			

Against your four spades, West cashes the ace and king of diamonds and switches to a club. You play low from dummy and East plays the ten. What is the best line of play?

Solution 53

Love All. Dealer North.

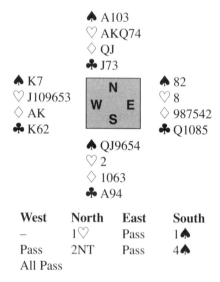

♠ A103
♡ AKQ74
◇ QJ
♣ J73

♠ K7
♡ J109653
◇ AK
♣ K62

♠ 82
♡ 8
◇ 987542
♣ Q1085

♠ QJ9654
♡ 2
◇ 1063
♣ A94

West	North	East	South
–	1♡	Pass	1♠
Pass	2NT	Pass	4♠
All Pass			

Against your four spades, West cashes the ace and king of diamonds and switches to a club. You play low from dummy and East plays the ten. What is the best line of play?

It seems clear to win the ace of clubs and play off dummy's hearts to discard clubs from your hand. The real issue is whether or not you should cash the ace of trumps before embarking on this play.

Cashing the ace of spades first gains when either (a) the bare king of spades drops, or (b) someone is now forced to ruff the *third* heart with the king of spades. You are always down if someone ruffs the *second* heart for they make a spade and a club.

Playing on hearts immediately gains when either (a) East ruffs the *second* heart with a small spade, or (b) he ruffs the *third* heart either with a small spade or the king. If East ruffs in on the hearts you can overruff and take the spade finesse. This is the better line and certainly works here.

So, win the ace of clubs and play off your top hearts. In the event, East ruffs the second heart with the eight of spades. You overruff but now need the spade finesse for your contract. When it is right, you can draw trumps, and discard one club loser on the remaining top heart.

The received wisdom in the above circumstances is to cash the trump ace before taking the discards but we have seen a number of hands recently where this is not the best line.

Problem 54

Love All Dealer West.

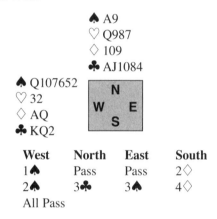

	♠ A9		
	♡ Q987		
	◇ 109		
	♣ AJ1084		

♠ Q107652
♡ 32
◇ AQ
♣ KQ2

West	North	East	South
1♠	Pass	Pass	2◇
2♠	3♣	3♠	4◇
All Pass			

You lead the six of spades which declarer wins in the dummy and runs the ten of diamonds. Over to you…

Solution 54

Love All Dealer West.

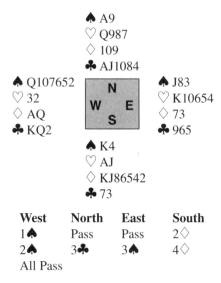

```
                    ♠ A9
                    ♡ Q987
                    ◇ 109
                    ♣ AJ1084
    ♠ Q107652         N         ♠ J83
    ♡ 32                         ♡ K10654
    ◇ AQ          W       E      ◇ 73
    ♣ KQ2              S         ♣ 965
                    ♠ K4
                    ♡ AJ
                    ◇ KJ86542
                    ♣ 73
```

West	North	East	South
1♠	Pass	Pass	2◇
2♠	3♣	3♠	4◇
All Pass			

You lead the six of spades which declarer wins in the dummy and runs the ten of diamonds. Over to you...

Because you have read about it in books like this you contemplate winning the diamond with the ace, although you cannot see how this will help. However, since declarer is unlikely to have a eight-card diamond suit it can hardly cost to win the ace and declarer will no doubt go back to dummy to repeat the finesse. Ah, there is the answer as to why you perpetrated this spot of deception in the first place. Declarer will now use up one of dummy's entries to repeat what you know to be a losing finesse. That is what happened here. You won the ace of diamonds and continued with another spade won by declarer who crossed to the ace of clubs as you played the queen. He repeated the diamond finesse which you won and exited with yet another spade. Declarer ruffed but had no entry to dummy to take the winning heart finesse.

Croatia were one down in five diamonds in the other room but in this room Ireland as North/South stopped in four diamonds and looked set for a gain of 5 IMPs until Marinkovic as West indeed won with the ace of diamonds. Flat board.

Problem 55

Game All. Dealer South.

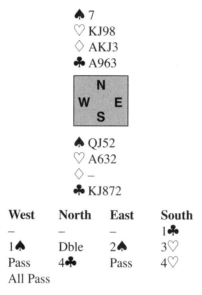

♠ 7
♡ KJ98
◇ AKJ3
♣ A963

♠ QJ52
♡ A632
◇ –
♣ KJ872

West	North	East	South
–	–	–	1♣
1♠	Dble	2♠	3♡
Pass	4♣	Pass	4♡
All Pass			

Against your four hearts West leads the two of diamonds. Plan the play.

Solution 55

Game All. Dealer South.

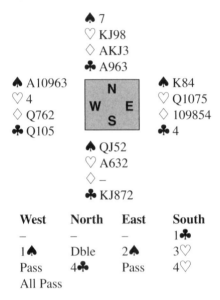

♠ 7
♡ KJ98
◇ AKJ3
♣ A963

♠ A10963
♡ 4
◇ Q762
♣ Q105

♠ K84
♡ Q1075
◇ 109854
♣ 4

♠ QJ52
♡ A632
◇ –
♣ KJ872

West	North	East	South
–	–	–	1♣
1♠	Dble	2♠	3♡
Pass	4♣	Pass	4♡
All Pass			

Against your four hearts West leads the two of diamonds. Plan the play.

On this type of hand it is very hard to add up your losers or your winners because you do not know how anything breaks. All you can do is say that there is some danger of losing one spade, two hearts and a club. If the queen of diamonds is right, which looks likely on the lead, you have three pitches for your clubs but if you are not going to develop the club suit you need to be sure you can come to enough tricks.

The spade layout on this deal is one that crops up quite often. The bidding has been very revealing. What do you know about the layout of the spade suit?

Presumably the honours are split because West would have led one had he had both the ace and king and would probably not have overcalled had he had neither. It is also extremely likely that West has five cards in the suit and East three. If this is the case you can generate a trick in the spade suit by playing a low spade from the dummy. If East goes in with his honour, you can take a ruffing finesse against West; if East plays low, two spade ruffs will bring down his honour.

At trick one play the jack of diamonds, which holds the trick as you throw a club. Now a spade to the queen and ace. West plays another spade. You ruff in the dummy, play the king of hearts and a heart to your ace and ruff a spade, dropping East's king. Now cash dummy's diamonds discarding the losing clubs and play clubs. East can take his two trump tricks whenever he likes but you have made your game with one spade, three diamonds, two clubs, two high hearts and two ruffs in dummy. The bad lie in hearts and clubs did not force you to go down.

Problem 56

Game All. Dealer South.

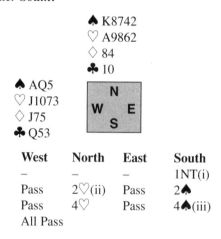

```
                    ♠ K8742
                    ♡ A9862
                    ◇ 84
                    ♣ 10
        ♠ AQ5       ┌─────────┐
        ♡ J1073     │    N    │
        ◇ J75       │ W     E │
        ♣ Q53       │    S    │
                    └─────────┘
```

West	North	East	South
–	–	–	1NT(i)
Pass	2♡(ii)	Pass	2♠
Pass	4♡	Pass	4♠(iii)
All Pass			

(i) 15–17   (ii) transfer, showing 5 spades   (iii) after a long pause

Because of declarer's long pause before choosing four spades, you guessed he would be 3-3 in the majors. Consequently you decided to lead a heart in the hope of giving partner a ruff.

The low heart lead goes to partner's queen and declarer's king. Declarer now played the jack of spades which you won with the ace and pressed on with your plan by continuing with a second low heart, won by dummy's ace as partner followed suit. Declarer continued with a diamond to his ace (your partner following with the nine) and the ten of spades. What do you know about the hand and how do you defend?

Solution 56

Game All. Dealer South.

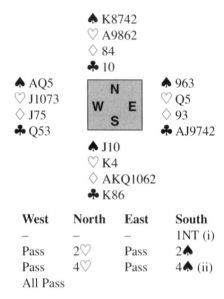

♠ K8742
♡ A9862
◇ 84
♣ 10

♠ AQ5
♡ J1073
◇ J75
♣ Q53

♠ 963
♡ Q5
◇ 93
♣ AJ9742

♠ J10
♡ K4
◇ AKQ1062
♣ K86

West	North	East	South
–	–	–	1NT (i)
Pass	2♡	Pass	2♠
Pass	4♡	Pass	4♠ (ii)
All Pass			

(i) 15–17   (ii) transfer, showing 5 spades   (iii) after a long pause

Against four spades you decided to lead a heart in the hope of giving partner a ruff. The heart lead went to partner's queen and declarer's king. Declarer now played the jack of spades which you won with the ace and continued with a second low heart, won by dummy's ace as partner followed suit. Declarer continued with a diamond to his ace (your partner following with the nine) and the ten of spades. What do you know about the hand and how do you defend?

If declarer is not 3-3 in the majors, presumably he is 2-2, else why the thought? Partner's nine of diamonds is consistent with a doubleton, giving declarer a 2-2-6-3 distribution, not so unlikely for a fourth-in-hand strong no-trump. So, if you cover the ten of spades with your queen, you will set up a trick for partner's nine. Is that then what you are going to do?

If you do, declarer will have little option but to give your partner his nine of spades and, as you have no entry for your heart tricks, declarer will surely succeed by taking whatever tricks he has in the minors.

Look at the effect of not covering the ten of spades. Declarer cannot overtake with dummy's king and play another round of spades for you would cash two heart tricks. All he can do is set about diamonds. Partner ruffs the third round and plays the jack of clubs (ace and another would do on this layout, but the jack would be better if declarer had the queen as well as the king). Declarer wins his king and plays a fourth diamond but you ruff with the queen, leaving him with two heart losers in the dummy.

This defence was found at the table by Margaret Courtney, one of our newest internationals, who was part of the English women's team that won the European Championships in 2001.

Problem 57

Love All. Dealer East.

♠ KJ2
♡ AJ5
♢ 72
♣ 86432

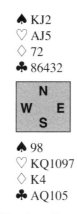

♠ 98
♡ KQ1097
♢ K4
♣ AQ105

West	North	East	South
–	–	1♢	1♡
Pass	2♡	Pass	3♣
Pass	4♡	All Pass	

Against your pushy four hearts, West leads the queen of diamonds to East's ace. East returns the king of clubs. Plan the play.

Solution 57

Love All. Dealer East.

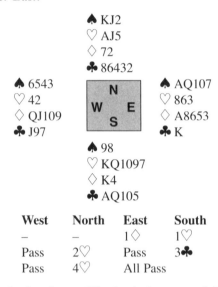

♠ KJ2
♡ AJ5
◇ 72
♣ 86432

♠ 6543
♡ 42
◇ QJ109
♣ J97

♠ AQ107
♡ 863
◇ A8653
♣ K

♠ 98
♡ KQ1097
◇ K4
♣ AQ105

West	North	East	South
–	–	1◇	1♡
Pass	2♡	Pass	3♣
Pass	4♡	All Pass	

Against your pushy four hearts, West leads the queen of diamonds to East's ace. East returns the king of clubs. Plan the play.

First, consider what will happen if you make the normal play of winning the ace of clubs and drawing trumps. Now you need to go to work on the club suit. You will cash the queen and if East started with Kx everything will be fine, but what if his king was a singleton? Now West will win the third round of clubs and switch to a spade through dummy's king. East must have the ace for his opening bid.

One of the key things to consider when planning the play of a hand is whether you can keep the danger hand off lead. Here, in the fullness of time, you will be able to discard one of your spades on dummy's long club, so, provided West does not gain the lead and switch to a spade, you will succeed. What you should do is *duck* the king of clubs at trick two (playing the ten, otherwise the suit is blocked). The only time this can go wrong is if East has found an inspired switch from Kxx. Should that happen all you can do is congratulate him – always be prepared to lose to genius!

After you have ducked the king of clubs and won whatever suit East switches to, you draw trumps and play your clubs from the top, eventually discarding a spade from hand on dummy's long club and claiming your contract with five hearts, one diamond and four club tricks. If East began with a doubleton club you have squandered an overtrick, but your primary concern should be making your contract.

Problem 58

Game All. Dealer South.

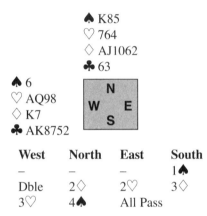

♠ K85
♡ 764
◇ AJ1062
♣ 63

♠ 6
♡ AQ98
◇ K7
♣ AK8752

West	North	East	South
–	–	–	1♠
Dble	2◇	2♡	3◇
3♡	4♠	All Pass	

Against South's four spades you lead a top club on which partner plays the jack and declarer the queen. Since cashing a second club looks to be the best hope of beating the game, at trick two you try a second top club, but declarer ruffs. Can you see any chance for the defence?

Solution 58

Game All. Dealer South.

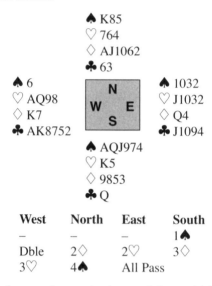

♠ K85
♡ 764
◇ AJ1062
♣ 63

♠ 6
♡ AQ98
◇ K7
♣ AK8752

♠ 1032
♡ J1032
◇ Q4
♣ J1094

♠ AQJ974
♡ K5
◇ 9853
♣ Q

West	North	East	South
–	–	–	1♠
Dble	2◇	2♡	3◇
3♡	4♠	All Pass	

Against South's four spades you lead a top club on which partner plays the jack and declarer the queen. Since cashing a second club looks to be the best hope of beating the game, at trick two you try a second top club, but declarer ruffs. Can you see any chance for the defence?

It looks as if declarer is cold. Maybe you could have taken two heart tricks earlier, but now declarer will surely draw trumps and finesse your king of diamonds, eventually discarding some heart losers on dummy's long diamond(s). Is there any hope at all?

There is just the small chance that partner has the queen of diamonds. If partner can get the lead with it he will be able to lead a heart through declarer, which will give you two heart tricks to go with your two minor-suit tricks. If partner has the queen of diamonds, do you need to do anything?

Declarer is surely about to draw trumps and play a diamond. If you play low he will rise with the ace and play a second round of the suit to your king (an avoidance play). With your hand on lead you will not be able to take two heart tricks. It would be better defence for you to insert your king but declarer can still succeed by ducking. Then on the next round of the suit he can rise with the ace dropping your partner's queen.

The way to guarantee success is for you to discard your king of diamonds on the second round of trumps. Now, perhaps a really clued-up declarer should have played diamonds before trumps, but just be thankful that your declarer did not!

Problem 59

Game All. Dealer North.

♠ K86
♡ A76
◇ AJ53
♣ J94

♠ AQJ104
♡ KQ104
◇ 6
♣ A76

West	North	East	South
–	1◇	Pass	1♠
Pass	1NT(i)	Pass	2♣(ii)
Pass	2♠	Pass	4NT(iii)
Pass	5♣(iv)	Pass	5♠
Pass	6♠	All Pass	

(i) 12–14   (ii) checkback, asking about North's distribution
(iii) Roman Key Card Blackwood   (iv) 0 or 3 aces (from 5)

Against your six spades, West leads the three of trumps. Can you see a way to make your sporting slam?

Solution 59

Game All. Dealer North.

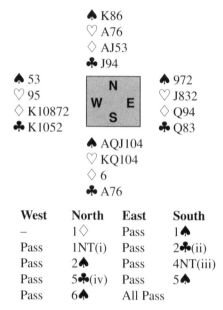

♠ K86
♡ A76
◇ AJ53
♣ J94

♠ 53
♡ 95
◇ K10872
♣ K1052

♠ 972
♡ J832
◇ Q94
♣ Q83

♠ AQJ104
♡ KQ104
◇ 6
♣ A76

West	North	East	South
–	1◇	Pass	1♠
Pass	1NT(i)	Pass	2♣(ii)
Pass	2♠	Pass	4NT(iii)
Pass	5♣(iv)	Pass	5♠
Pass	6♠	All Pass	

(i) 12–14   (ii) checkback, asking about North's distribution
(iii) Roman Key Card Blackwood   (iv) 0 or 3 aces (from 5)

Against your six spades, West leads the three of trumps. Can you see a way to make your sporting slam?

You have rather overbid here, as partner's hand is quite suitable and the slam is far from straightforward. This deal is a good example of playing for the precise distribution that you need.

You can count five spade tricks, four heart tricks (hopefully), one diamond and one club. It is hard to see where the twelfth can possibly come from. Sometimes this type of hand can succeed by ruffing three diamonds in your hand but here you do not have the entries for such a play (a 'dummy reversal').

Can you see that your only chance is to ruff a club in the dummy? To do this you need to play four rounds of hearts from your hand discarding a club from dummy and then ruff your club loser. The trouble with this idea, though, is that one of the defenders is likely to ruff your fourth heart trick. You need to hope that hearts are 4-2 and that the defender with a doubleton heart has only a doubleton trump.

So… win the trump in hand and duck a club. Win the trump return, cash the king of hearts, play a heart to the ace and then a heart to your ten (they need to break 4-2 for you to make your contract, remember). Now cash the queen of hearts discarding a club from dummy, cash the ace of clubs and ruff a club. Now return to hand with a diamond ruff to draw the last trump. Well played.

This deal was originally played by that great Brazilian player, Gabriel Chagas, and reported by Phillip Alder.

Problem 60

Love All. Dealer South.

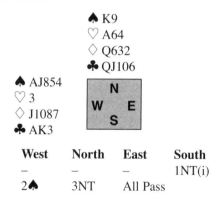

♠ K9
♡ A64
◇ Q632
♣ QJ106

♠ AJ854
♡ 3
◇ J1087
♣ AK3

West	North	East	South
–	–	–	1NT(i)
2♠	3NT	All Pass	

(i) 14–16

Against South's three no-trumps you lead your fourth-highest spade, the five. The king is played from dummy and your partner plays the two indicating an odd number. Declarer now cashes the ace and king of diamonds (partner playing the nine followed by the four), followed by the ace and king of hearts (partner playing the two followed by the eight). You have no choice but to discard a low club. Declarer now plays a club. Over to you.

Solution 60

Love All. Dealer South.

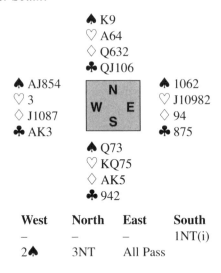

♠ K9
♡ A64
♢ Q632
♣ QJ106

♠ AJ854
♡ 3
♢ J1087
♣ AK3

♠ 1062
♡ J10982
♢ 94
♣ 875

♠ Q73
♡ KQ75
♢ AK5
♣ 942

West	North	East	South
–	–	–	1NT(i)
2♠	3NT	All Pass	

(i) 14–16

Against South's three no-trumps you lead your fourth-highest spade, the five. The king is played from dummy and your partner plays the two indicating an odd number. Declarer now cashes the ace and king of diamonds (partner playing the nine followed by the four), followed by the ace and king of hearts (partner playing the two followed by the eight). You have no choice but to discard a low club. Declarer now plays a club. Over to you.

What is going on? There is no room for partner to have more than a jack so it looks as if the complete deal is as it is. You may think it looks as though you can afford to play a low spade, giving declarer another spade trick. After all, that will only bring his total up to eight: three in each red suit and two spades. When you get in with your second top club you will have three spades to cash. The problem with that is that declarer will win the queen of spades and play another heart. What will you discard? You can't afford to throw a diamond, so will have to throw a spade. Now when you get in with your other top club you will have only two spades to cash.

Partner may not have very much but the card you need to play him for is the ten of spades – a pretty likely card, actually, since with Q10x declarer would have run your five to his hand at trick one – and some good hearts.

You must win the first club and exit with the *jack* of spades. Declarer can win with the queen and cash the queen of hearts, as suggested above, and you will discard a spade. But now, when declarer plays a second club you can win with the ace and play a *low* spade to partner's ten. Partner has two good hearts to cash. Despite your 13 HCP and his solitary HCP, he will take three defensive tricks and you only two.

HAND CATEGORISATION

Rather than present an index in the normal fashion, it seemed more helpful to categorise the hands so the reader can easily look for problems of a particular type. The numbers refer to the number of the problem rather than the number of the page.

attitude signal 19
avoidance play 21, 25, 40, 48, 57, 58
avoiding an endplay 22, 24, 37
bidding problems 14, 39, 49, 51
blocking and unblocking 1, 6, 8, 42, 58
combining chances 13, 41, 44
counting losers 17
counting tricks 4, 19
crocodile coup 45
cutting communications 18, 35, 42, 43, 47, 52
danger hand 21, 40, 57, 58
deception 54
don't finesse 17
ducking 25, 29, 46, 57
elimination play 5, 46
endplay 29, 46
entry problems 7, 8, 36, 45, 56
finesse 7, 11, 34, 48

forcing defence 30
handling trumps 20
helping partner 26
maintaining communications 28, 60
only chance 7, 59
opening leads 10, 30, 50
overtaking play 33
percentages 27
preventing ruffs 2
safety play 3, 9, 11, 46
signalling 41
squeeze 37, 60
suit preference 15
throw-in 5, 46
timing in defence 16, 31, 47
timing in dummy play 17, 23, 36, 53, 55
trump control 32, 34, 38, 53, 56
trump promotion 12, 24, 33
vital switch 4